THE ECONOMICS OF
WELFARE POLICIES

MARGARET S. GORDON

COLUMBIA UNIVERSITY PRESS

New York and London

TO BOB AND DAVE

FOREWORD

This work is one of a series of three dealing with the economics of health, education, and welfare. In commissioning these books, the Foundation was influenced by the fact that expenditures in these three fields are in excess of $100 billion annually, that they are among the most important and sensitive areas of the entire economy, and that communication between economists and those making policy and operating decisions in these areas has been infrequent and irregular.

Dr. Margaret S. Gordon is a distinguished economist who has had a long-standing interest in welfare problems. As Associate Director of the Institute of Industrial Relations at the University of California, Berkeley, and as editor of *Industrial Relations*, she has made important contributions to the subject and was therefore a logical choice to undertake a review of past work and to suggest future research opportunities. It is hoped that this volume will prove of value to administrators of welfare programs, social workers, legislators charged with determining the amount and direction of flow of public funds to welfare, and others with similar interests and responsibilities. This book will certainly not solve all their problems or answer all their questions, but it may open up new lines of thought and provide an introduction to the light that economics can throw on problems of welfare. Dr. Gordon's colleagues within the economics profession will appreciate her succinct and knowledgeable review of the literature and may find themselves stimulated to make their own research contributions to this vital area of public policy.

The other two works in the series are *The Economic Value of Education* by Professor T. W. Schultz, of the University of Chicago, and *The Economics of Health* by Professor Herbert Klarman, of Johns Hopkins University. All three authors have been free to develop and interpret the materials in their chosen field according to their own judgment; the views expressed are, of course, their own. The Ford Foundation is grateful to them for the time and care that they have devoted to this important task.

Henry H. Villard, Director
Program in Economic Development
and Administration

May, 1963
New York City

PREFACE

This book would undoubtedly be a great deal longer had I known from the start that it would be published as a separate volume. It is probably just as well that I did not know. Its purpose is to stimulate interest in the economic issues associated with welfare policies, and to call attention to some of the important unsettled questions, rather than to provide an exhaustive discussion of all the problems.

I am indebted to Dr. Ida C. Merriam, Director, and Lenore A. Epstein, Assistant Director, Division of Research and Statistics, U. S. Social Security Administration, for their helpful critical comments on an earlier draft. The comments of Dr. Victor R. Fuchs of the Ford Foundation were also useful. It was a decided advantage, at various stages of the work, to be married to an economist whose knowledge of the literature in the field is extensive and who was able, in a number of instances, to steer me to a particularly useful article or volume. As always, moreover, my husband's critical comments on the manuscript were especially valuable.

Although this project was sponsored by the Ford Foundation, the Institute of Industrial Relations at the University of California, Berkeley, provided substantial support for my research. I am indebted to Dr. Marjorie S. Galenson, Malcolm Gutter, and Joyce Brown of the Institute staff for assistance at various stages of the study. My secretary, Joan Lewis, displayed admirable patience through several retypings of text, tables, and the long list of references.

It is scarcely necessary to add that I alone am responsible for the views expressed in the volume, as well as for any errors or omissions.

December 17, 1962   Margaret S. Gordon
Berkeley, California

CONTENTS

THE ECONOMICS OF
WELFARE POLICIES

INTRODUCTION

Throughout most of recorded history, society has assumed some degree of responsibility for the relief of poverty, but, whereas in earlier periods private organizations played the leading role in providing benefits for the poor, the modern tendency has been for governments to assume an increasing share of the responsibility. The factors accounting for this trend are complex. Underlying the whole development is the process of industrialization, with its manifold social and economic consequences. However, increasing governmental intervention in the welfare field began long before the industrial revolution and is manifest today in countries that have scarcely been touched by industrialization.

Historically, we may distinguish three stages in the development of public welfare programs. The breakdown of feudalism and, somewhat later, the Reformation led to the adoption of public systems of poor relief, largely at the local level, to replace, at least in part, the welfare functions carried out by church, manor, and guild in medieval society (62, 81). However, although the transition from feudalism to the market-oriented economies of the sixteenth and seventeenth centuries was accompanied by an increase in economic insecurity for the working classes, prevailing social views regarded poverty as largely a result of individual shiftlessness—except in the case of the aged, the disabled, and needy children, who were classified as impotent or dependent. Standards of poor relief were harshly restrictive and meager, lest able-bodied persons be encouraged not to work.

During the course of the nineteenth century, as the effects of the industrial revolution became increasingly apparent in western Europe, more sophisticated views of the causes of poverty gradually developed, and in this highly significant change economists played an important role. Industrial wage-earners came to be regarded as a group whose income security was jeopardized by the economic and social risks of unemployment, disability, and old age, largely as a result of forces beyond their control. Moreover, particularly in the early part of the century, prevailing wage theories held out little hope for a rise in the real income of the working classes. In this environment the socialist movement gained strength, and it remained for a shrewd politician, Chancellor Bismarck, to adopt a strategy designed to stave off socialism by protecting the wage-earner from the economic risks of modern industrial life through social insurance programs. Increasingly, during the next half-century, the German social insurance laws of the 1880s influenced the course of welfare legislation in other countries and gradually pushed the older forms of poor relief into a subordinate position.

A third stage in the development of modern attitudes toward public welfare has been associated with the Keynesian "revolution," with its emphasis on fiscal policy as a central tool in the maintenance of full employment. Although older humanitarian and social considerations continue to play a role, public welfare programs have also come to be regarded as part of a battery of instruments available to the modern state in its efforts to maintain economic stability. This attitude has clearly played a significant role in connection with the marked expansion and liberalization of social security programs which has characterized the period since World War II.

It may be that we are on the threshold of a fourth stage, associated with the rising concern about economic growth. Increasing emphasis on the importance of manpower goals and policies designed to bring about the full development and utilization of human resources is leading to renewed interest in the relationship of welfare programs to the maintenance of the health and efficiency of the population. This aspect of welfare programs was by no means ignored by classical and neoclassical economists, but it tended to receive relatively little attention in the Keynesian literature. Recently, however, there has been a substantial revival of interest in the relationship of "investment in human resources" to economic growth. It should also be noted that the impact of welfare programs on health and efficiency has tended to receive considerable attention in totalitarian societies.

This brief historical sketch suggests, but does not fully spell out, the reasons for government intervention in the welfare field. These include: 1) the inability of private welfare organizations to carry the entire burden, particularly in time of depression; 2) the difficulty of achieving equitable treatment of all the victims of poverty through private channels; 3) the absence of organized relief agencies in rural areas; 4) the inverse relationship between income and the incidence of the economic and social risks associated with modern industrial life, with the result that those most likely to incur these risks can least afford to protect themselves through private saving and private insurance; 5) the influence, particularly from the eighteenth century onward, of egalitarian ideologies; 6) growing recognition of the fact that poverty and slum conditions entail social costs for the entire community; and 7) other factors already mentioned, such as the influence of Keynesian economics.

Nevertheless, there has been a surprising lack of interest in public welfare policies on the part of American economists in the period since World War II. Although economists were prominent in the deliberations that led to the adoption of the Social Security Act of 1935, and participated actively in debates over various aspects of social insurance in the late 1930s, there has been, with a few exceptions, relative indifference to the development of public policy in this area in the postwar period. On the whole, this appears to have been less true in western Europe than in the United States. In a postwar environment which for more than a decade was dominated by high employment levels and inflationary trends, the attention of American economists was largely turned elsewhere. In the last few years, however, as concern over the problem of long-term unemployment and a slug-

gish rate of economic growth has increased, there have been
signs of a reawakening interest in the economics profession with
regard to welfare programs.

The neglect of this important aspect of applied economics
has left the professional literature in an unsatisfactory state—
particularly in the United States, but also, in some respects, in
western Europe. Although the role of certain welfare programs,
particularly unemployment insurance, as "automatic stabilizers"
has received frequent mention, the question as to whether the
whole complex constellation of American public welfare programs
is adequately designed to contribute to economic stability has
received relatively little attention. Scanty attention has been
paid, also, to the impact of welfare programs on consumption,
saving, investment, and economic growth. And one would search
practically in vain among the writings of American economists
for any analysis of the problems facing underdeveloped areas in
developing welfare programs, despite the intense interest in
problems of economic development.

The purpose of this volume is to discuss some of the major
economic issues associated with welfare programs, with particular reference to the treatment of these issues in the economics
literature. I shall be less concerned with exhaustive analysis
than with an attempt to call attention to important unsettled
questions, in the hope that research will thus be stimulated.

Welfare programs will be defined as social programs designed to transfer income, in cash, in kind, or in the form of
services, to those whose capacity for self-support has been impaired, interrupted, or (in the case of children) has not yet
reached maturity. To a large extent, we shall be dealing with
programs involving transfers from earners to nonearners. Both
public and private (philanthropic) welfare programs are included
in this definition, but private programs will not be analyzed,
largely because their significance for the economy is relatively
minor as compared with public programs. As we shall see, the
total expenditures involved are very much smaller. Our definition
does not include employee benefit plans, since they are regarded
as privately sponsored programs to benefit particular groups of

employees—providing benefits that are often referred to as deferred wages—rather than social programs designed to transfer income from one group to another. Because of the highly important relationships between social security programs and private employee benefit plans, however, plans of the latter type will enter the discussion at certain points.

Health and education are often included in definitions of social welfare programs, e.g., in the highly useful statistics prepared by Ida C. Merriam of the Social Security Administration. They will be excluded from our definition, however, largely because there have been a number of recent studies of the economics of health and education. In other words, we shall be dealing almost entirely with income-maintenance programs, although certain public subsidy programs designed to benefit low-income consumers will also be included.

Any attempt to discuss the economic issues associated with every public welfare program in the United States would be well beyond the scope of this study. I propose, therefore, to trace the growth of public welfare expenditures, refer briefly to private welfare expenditures, compare public welfare expenditures in this country with those in foreign countries, and present some data on the income-redistribution effects of welfare programs. Then, for purposes of a more intensive treatment of economic issues in the welfare field, I shall consider the economics of two major American public welfare programs—OASDI and unemployment insurance. These two programs are exceedingly important in terms both of their scope and their economic significance. Although this procedure has some drawbacks, it will have the advantage of making the discussion more meaningful to persons who are not sufficiently familiar with the details of individual programs to grasp the relevance of a more general discussion of economic issues to particular program provisions. The OASDI and unemployment insurance programs are described in an appendix, for the benefit of readers who are not particularly familiar with them.

1. WELFARE PROGRAMS IN THE UNITED STATES

Under the impact of mass unemployment, the proportion of the national income spent on public welfare programs rose to an unprecedented peak in the Great Depression of the 1930s. Although detailed data are lacking, it would appear that public welfare expenditures, as we have defined them, amounted only to between 1 and 2 percent of the national income in the 1920s, and that the largest expenditures were for veterans' benefits (73). By 1934-35, the first year for which detailed estimates are available, total public welfare expenditures amounted to nearly $4 billion, or 7.3 percent of a greatly shrunken national income (see Table 1). By far the largest item, representing more than three-fifths of the total, was "other public aid," which included chiefly earnings from work relief and emergency public work programs. [1]

Five years later, unemployment had declined from its depression peak but still amounted to about 15 percent of the civilian labor force. Public welfare expenditures, though larger in dollar terms, were down to 6.8 percent of the national income, but "other public aid" still represented by far the largest item, or

[1] It should be noted that expenditures on public work programs, and to some extent on work relief programs, do not conform to a strict definition of transfer payments, since they are payments for productive services, but we have chosen not to exclude them since their increase in the thirties was brought on almost entirely by a desire to meet the unemployment problem, and these expenditures were considerably heavier than they might have been if such programs as old-age insurance and unemployment insurance had existed at the beginning of the depression.

nearly half of the total. Public assistance had grown to more than a fifth, while unemployment insurance and the public employment service amounted to about a tenth. Payments under old-age and survivors insurance had barely begun and represented a tiny fraction of the total.

World War II, with its tight manpower situation, gave rise to a drop in public welfare expenditures, which by 1944-45 amounted to only 1.8 percent of a greatly increased national income. In 1949-50, expenditures were substantially higher, and there was a change in the distribution of expenditures associated with postwar developments and with the fact that the year was one of moderately heavy unemployment.

By 1960-61, public welfare expenditures were up to 7.5 percent of the national income and had been rising fairly steadily. By far the most important factor in the postwar expansion of these expenditures had been the growth of social insurance programs, which by the early sixties represented 70 percent of the total. Dominating this development was the expansion of the Old Age, Survivors, and Disability Insurance program, which by 1960-61 was providing benefits for nearly two-thirds of all persons aged 65 and over, as well as for large numbers of younger persons who were receiving survivors or disability benefits.[2] Unemployment insurance expenditures fluctuated in relative importance with changes in the unemployment rate, while expenditures on other social insurance and minor welfare programs—now more varied in scope and character than in the 1930s—tended to represent a fairly constant share of the total. On the other hand, public assistance expenditures and veterans' benefits, though somewhat higher in dollar terms than in the late 1940s, had declined sharply as a percent of the total.

Although the provision of poor relief was largely left to the local governments until the Great Depression, federal government welfare expenditures apparently exceeded those of state and local governments in the 1920s, reflecting the relative importance of expenditures on veterans' programs. The story of the break-

[2]A significant number of women in the 62-64 age group were also receiving actuarially reduced old-age benefits.

Table 1

PUBLIC WELFARE EXPENDITURES IN THE UNITED STATES, BY TYPE OF PROGRAM AND AS PERCENT OF NATIONAL INCOME, SELECTED YEARS, 1934-35 TO 1960-61

Type of program or item	1934-35	1939-40	1944-45	1949-50	1956-57	1957-58	1958-59	1959-60	1960-61
Social insurance	8.3	21.3	38.1	43.3	63.4	66.8	68.2	68.5	69.6
Old-age, survivors and disability insurance		0.5	8.2	7.4	35.0	35.3	36.7	40.1	38.6
Railroad retirement		2.2	4.4	2.9	3.5	3.1	3.0	3.4	3.2
Public employee retirement	5.5	4.8	11.7	7.0	9.4	8.7	9.0	9.3	9.1
Unemployment insurance and employment service		10.4	5.0	19.8	9.7	14.2	14.2	10.3	13.7
State temporary disability service			0.2	0.7	1.3	1.2	1.1	1.1	1.1
Workmen's compensation	2.8	3.0	8.5	4.1	3.8	3.3	3.2	3.3	3.0
Other insurance programs[a]		0.4	0.1	1.4	0.7	1.0	1.0	1.0	0.9
Public aid	78.0	67.9	31.5	23.6	15.8	14.1	13.7	13.1	12.3
Public assistance	16.2	21.2	31.4	23.5	15.5	13.8	13.3	12.9	11.9
Other[b]	61.8	46.7	0.1	0.1	0.3	0.3	0.4	0.2	0.4
Other welfare services	3.6	2.2	5.9	3.7	4.0	3.8	3.8	4.2	3.9
Vocational rehabilitation	0.1	0.1	0.3	0.2	0.3	0.3	0.3	0.3	0.3
Institutional and other care	2.8	1.2	2.1	1.0	1.0	1.4	1.4	1.6	1.6
School lunch			1.4	1.5	1.9	1.3	1.4	1.5	1.3
Child welfare	0.7	0.9	2.1	1.0	0.8	0.8	0.7	0.8	0.7

Veterans' programs	10.1	8.5	24.2	29.4	16.2	14.7	13.7	13.6	13.6
Pensions and compensation	10.1	8.5	23.2	19.9	15.2	13.5	12.7	12.4	11.8
Welfare and other	—c	—c	1.0	9.5	1.0	1.2	1.0	1.2	1.8
Public housing	0.1	0.3	—c	0.6	0.6	0.6	0.6	0.6	0.6
Total (in millions of dollars)[d]	3,847	5,291	3,267	10,564	19,093	23,322	26,179	27,529	31,421
Total (as percent of national income)	7.3	6.9	1.7	4.8	5.3	6.4	6.8	6.7	7.5

[a] Includes railroad unemployment insurance and railroad temporary disability insurance.

[b] Includes work program earnings, other emergency aid programs, and value of surplus food distributed to needy persons.

[c] Less than 0.05 percent.

[d] All expenditures for medical care and education have been excluded.

Sources: Ida C. Merriam, "Social Welfare Expenditures, 1960–61," *Social Security Bulletin*, XXV (November, 1962), 4, and *Survey of Current Business*.

down of state, local, and private relief programs during the Great Depression and the development of massive federal works programs and other emergency relief measures is a familiar one. In 1934-35, federal programs accounted for three-fourths of all public welfare expenditures (see Table 2). By 1949-50, the federal government's share was down to 55 percent, but during the 1950s it gradually climbed back, so that by 1960-61 it amounted to nearly three-fourths of the total again. Clearly, the chief reason for this trend has been the development and expansion of the

Table 2

GROWTH OF FEDERAL AND STATE AND LOCAL PUBLIC WELFARE EXPENDITURES, DISTRIBUTION BY TYPE OF PROGRAM AND PERCENT OF TOTAL EXPENDITURES, SELECTED YEARS, 1934-35 TO 1960-61

Type of program or item	Federal			State and local		
	1934-35	*1949-50*	*1960-61*	*1934-35*	*1949-50*	*1960-61*
Social insurance	3.4	35.3	70.0	22.7	56.1	68.6
Old-age, survivors, and disability insurance		13.5	53.4			
Railroad retirement		5.2	4.3			
Public employee retirement	3.2	7.5	7.4	12.2	6.5	13.6
Unemployment insurance and employment service		6.2	3.5		39.4	40.9
State temporary disability insurance					1.5	3.9
Workmen's compensation	0.2	0.3	0.2	10.5	8.7	10.2
Other insurance programs[a]		2.6	1.2			
Public aid	82.9	19.0	9.1	63.4	29.3	20.6
Public assistance		18.9	8.5	63.4	29.3	20.6
Other[b]	82.9	0.1	0.6			
Other welfare services	0.1	2.8	1.9	13.9	4.9	9.4
Veterans' programs	13.6	42.7	18.3		9.7	1.0
Public housing		0.2	0.7			0.4

Table 2 (Continued)

Type of program or item	Federal			State and local		
	1934-35	1949-50	1960-61	1934-35	1949-50	1960-61
Total (in millions of dollars)^c	2,862	5,817	22,833	984	4,748	8,588
Percent of total public welfare expenditures	74.4	55.1	72.7	25.6	44.9	27.3
Welfare expenditures as percent of federal or state and local total expenditures	44.7	14.1	23.5	11.9	20.8	15.3

[a]Includes railroad unemployment insurance and railroad temporary disability insurance.

[b]Includes work program earnings, other emergency aid programs, and value of surplus food distributed to needy persons.

[c]All expenditures for medical care and education have been excluded.

Sources: Ida C. Merriam, "Social Welfare Expenditures, 1960-61," Social Security Bulletin, XXV (November, 1962), 5-6, and Economic Report of the President (Washington, D.C., Government Printing Office, annual).

OASDI program to its present predominant position in the public welfare scene, but other developments have played a role, particularly the sharp drop in state government expenditures on veterans' programs after the late 1940s.

There is little doubt that the federal share of public welfare expenditures will continue to rise. Expenditures on the OASDI program will go on increasing as the program continues to mature, even in the unlikely event that no further amendments of an expanding or liberalizing character are adopted. Veterans' expenditures, moreover, are expected to increase substantially in the 1960s, as more and more World War I veterans reach the age of 65 and take advantage of the possibility of applying for pensions for non-service-connected disabilities (115). Furthermore, under the provisions of the 1961 housing act, federal expenditures on housing will rise substantially.

On the other hand, programs administered by the states are less likely to show a sharp upward trend in expenditures. If the unemployment rate fails to decline substantially, the states will, of course, continue to bear rather heavy unemployment insurance expenditures, but the federal government's share of expenditures for the unemployed (particularly for retraining programs) will rise under recently enacted legislation. Meanwhile, both federal and state expenditures for such purposes as rehabilitation may be expected to rise.

By comparison with public expenditures for welfare purposes, private welfare expenditures represent a tiny proportion of

Table 3

PERCENTAGE DISTRIBUTION OF WELFARE EXPENDITURES
FROM PHILANTHROPIC CONTRIBUTIONS, BY PURPOSE OF
EXPENDITURES, AND TOTAL EXPENDITURES AS PERCENT OF
NATIONAL INCOME, UNITED STATES, SELECTED YEARS,
1930–55

Purpose	*1930*	*1940*	*1950*	*1955*
Church welfare	32.4	25.0	23.5	25.2
Secular welfare, services and care	67.7	75.0	70.5	67.8
Recreation, informal education, and group work	n.a.	n.a.	19.4	26.0
Family services and specialized care and services for children	n.a.	n.a.	32.4	23.9
Institutional care of adults	n.a.	n.a.	8.8	7.4
Services for handicapped, sheltered workshops, maternity home care, and other welfare services	n.a.	n.a.	10.0	10.4
Fund-raising and central administrative costs	n.a.	n.a.	5.9	7.0
Total (in millions of dollars)	247	200	850	1,150
Total (as percent of national income)	0.33	0.25	0.35	0.35

Source: Thomas Karter, "Voluntary Agency Expenditures for Health and Welfare from Philanthropic Contributions," *Social Security Bulletin,* XXI (February, 1958), 16.

the national income—only about 0.35 percent in 1955 (see Table 3). However, despite the marked expansion of public welfare expenditures since the 1920s, private welfare expenditures have tended to hold their own as a percentage of the national income. Undoubtedly, rising real income and the tax advantages associated with philanthropic giving have played an important role in explaining this tendency. Other factors have been continued urbanization (private welfare activities tend to be relatively limited in rural areas), the perception of new needs, and the professionalization of welfare services. The trend toward centralization of fund-raising under the auspices of broadly based community chests and, more recently, united area funds, has also had the effect, not only of facilitating well-organized publicity campaigns, but also, through the organization of labor-management committees and other employee collection committees, of encouraging contributions at the place of work by average income-receivers. Thus, the habit of philanthropic giving may be less confined to the wealthy sectors of the community than in earlier periods.

2. SOME INTERNATIONAL COMPARISONS

PUBLIC WELFARE EXPENDITURES

In European countries, as well as in the British Commonwealth, public welfare expenditures tend to represent an appreciably larger proportion of the national income than in the United States.

Highly useful for purposes of comparison, since they conform reasonably closely to our definition of public welfare expenditures, are the data on social security benefits and "other current transfers" in 15 countries published by the Organization for European Economic Cooperation. Conforming less closely to our definition, since they include payments to vendors of medical care under health insurance or health service programs, but nevertheless useful for comparisons embracing a larger number of countries, are data on social security expenditures prepared by the International Labour Office. In Table 4, the OEEC data for 1957 are included along with the ILO data for 1950, 1953, and 1957. It is apparent that the more highly industrialized countries tend to spend larger proportions of their national incomes on social security programs than underdeveloped areas. Among the more industrialized countries there is no very consistent relationship between national income per capita and the proportion of the national income represented by social security expenditures, although expenditures in such high-income countries as the United States, Canada, and Switzerland are considerably smaller in relation to the national income than in some of the countries with much lower per capita incomes, such as Austria and Italy.

Table 4

SOCIAL SECURITY EXPENDITURES, AS PERCENT OF
NATIONAL INCOME, SELECTED COUNTRIES, 1950, 1953, AND 1957

Geographical region and country	ILO data			OEEC data
	1950	*1953*	*1957*	*1957*
Western Europe				
Austria	15.4	19.0	17.6	14.6
Belgium	15.3	16.2	16.3	11.2
Denmark[a]	9.0	10.8	12.0	n.a.
Finland	8.9	10.9	12.0	
France	15.9	17.6	18.9	17.3
West Germany	20.3	19.4	20.8	17.3
Ireland[a]	8.3	9.2	11.5	8.1
Italy	10.7	13.4	15.2	13.2
The Netherlands	9.8	10.3	12.3	8.6
Norway[a]	7.4	8.8	10.1	7.3
Portugal	5.2	5.1	6.5	2.2
Sweden	10.4	10.8	12.9	7.4
Switzerland	6.6	7.3	8.7	
United Kingdom[a]	11.2	12.5	11.9	6.9
Eastern Europe				
Poland			7.7	
Yugoslavia		11.2	10.3	
North America				
Canada[a]	7.8	8.2	8.7	8.8
United States[a]	5.1	4.7	6.0	5.5
Central and South America				
Chile	7.6		9.7	
Guatemala[a]	1.5	3.0	3.1	
Australasia				
Australia[a]	7.4	8.3	9.1	
New Zealand[a]	14.1	13.2	13.0	
Asia				
Ceylon[a]	2.8	3.3	4.2	
China (Taiwan)	0.2	0.2	0.8	
India[a]			1.0	
Japan[a]		4.8	5.9	
Africa and Middle East				
Israel	5.7	5.9[a]	7.1[a]	

Table 4 (Continued)

Geographical region and country	ILO data 1950	ILO data 1953	ILO data 1957	OEEC data 1957
Tunisia		5.5	5.7	
Turkey	1.7	1.1	1.3	
Union of South Africa[a]	4.4	4.5	4.5	

[a]Data relate to fiscal years (1949-50, 1952-53, and 1956-57).

Sources: *The Cost of Social Security, 1949-1957* (Geneva, International Labour Office 1961), pp. 205-10; *Statistical Yearbook* (United Nations, annual); *Statistics of Sources and Uses of Finances, 1948-1958* (Paris, Organization for European Economic Cooperation, 1960), Table 2. See the text for an explanation of the differences between the ILO and OEEC data.

However, there appears to be some tendency for the countries with the oldest social ʻsecurity programs of a relatively modern type (social insurance and general old-age pension programs) to maintain comparatively high benefit levels in their social security programs and also to spend relatively large amounts on them as a percentage of national income.[1]

There has also been a tendency for the proportion of the national income represented by public welfare payments to rise during the 1950s. For the most part, moreover, these increases have been associated with expansion and liberalization of the programs.[2] And in some countries, the increases that occurred after

[1]In an analysis of data for 18 industrial countries, for example, I found a significant and fairly high correlation between the date of establishment of an old-age pension program for a sizable segment of the population and the level of average benefits (under old-age, survivors, and invalidity programs) measured as a percentage of national per capita income, the countries with the oldest programs ranking highest in benefit levels (109). On the Danish experience, see an article by Henning Friis (63). It should be noted, of course, that, in long-term insurance programs, expenditures tend to increase as the schemes mature and increasing numbers of persons become eligible for benefits.

[2]For information on social security developments, see the useful articles which appear frequently in 214, 219, 220, and 222. See, also, 61, 67, 80, and 86.

1956-57 were not explained to any substantial extent by increased unemployment, as they were in the United States.[3]

Some of the countries with comparatively high social security expenditures—notably France—devote sizable amounts to family allowance systems in relation to their national incomes (see Table 5). It is interesting to note, in this connection that although family allowance systems are widespread,[4] the differences in proportions of national income spent on these programs are strikingly wide, and there is some tendency for countries with large Catholic populations to have the highest relative expenditures.

Variations in percentages spent on public employee benefit systems are also wide and reflect, at least in part, substantial differences in the scope of public activities in various countries, particularly the extent to which industries are nationalized.[5] Differences in proportions expended on public health services are, also, partly explained by the extent to which health services have been nationalized. The United Kingdom, for example, which shifted from a compulsory national health insurance system to a national health service after World War II, ranks well above the other countries represented in Table 5 in the proportion of its national income spent on public health services. Its comparatively modest social insurance expenditures, on the other hand, are explained in part by the absence of health insurance expenditures—but only in part; Britain's flat social insurance benefits tend to be substantially lower in relation to average

[3]In West Germany, for example, a sharp rise between 1956 and 1958 was chiefly explained by an increase from 5.9 to 8.8 percent in the proportion of the national income represented by pension payments under the old-age and invalidity insurance program, which was greatly liberalized in 1957, whereas unemployment insurance and assistance payments represented only 1.1 percent of the national income in both years (89, p. 7).

[4]In 1961, 60 countries had family allowance systems (86, p. vii).

[5]There are also some variations in the extent to which employees of nationalized industries are covered by general social security programs or by special programs for public employees.

Table 5

SOCIAL SECURITY EXPENDITURES, BY TYPE OF PROGRAM, AS PERCENT OF NATIONAL INCOME, SELECTED COUNTRIES, 1957

Geographical region and country	Social Insurance and assimilated schemes	Family allowances	Public employers	Public health services	Public assistance and assimilated schemes	Benefits for war victims	Total[d]
Western Europe							
Austria	11.1	1.6	3.1	-c	1.0	1.2	17.6
Belgium	8.1	2.5	3.2	0.4	1.2	1.0	16.3
Denmark[a]	6.0	0.6	1.1	2.4	1.6	0.1	12.0
Finland	3.6	2.3	1.3	2.2	1.7	0.8	12.0
France	8.5	5.1	3.5	-	0.9	1.3	18.9
West Germany	13.7	0.3	3.3	0.1	1.6	2.3	20.8
Ireland[a]	5.5	1.2	1.3	2.8	0.6	-	11.5
Italy	7.3	3.2	2.8	0.2	0.4	1.7	15.2
The Netherlands	7.7	1.8	2.0	-	0.8	0.1	12.3
Norway[a]	5.3	0.6	1.7	1.4	1.0	0.1	10.1
Portugal	1.6	1.0	1.5	0.4	2.0	-c	6.5
Sweden	6.5	1.1	0.7	2.7	1.6	-	12.9
Switzerland	4.8	-c	1.1	1.5	1.4	-	8.7
United Kingdom[a]	4.7	0.7	0.7	4.3	1.6	0.6	12.1
Eastern Europe							
Poland[b]	2.6	2.3	0.2	2.4	...	0.1	7.7
Yugoslavia	6.3	3.0	-	0.6	0.1	0.6	10.3

North America							
Canada[a]	3.4	1.7	0.3	1.7	0.8	0.8	8.7
United States[a]	3.0	—	0.6	0.5	0.9	1.1	6.0
Central and South America							
Chile	3.0	3.0	3.4	0.4	—	—	9.7
Guatemala[a]	1.1	—	0.3	1.7	—	—	3.1
Australasia							
Australia[a]	5.8	—	0.5	1.2	0.2	1.4	9.1
New Zealand[a]	8.9	—	0.8	2.2	0.1	1.0	13.0
Asia							
Ceylon[a]	—[c]	—	1.3	2.1	0.8	—	4.2
China (Taiwan)	0.2	—	—[c]	0.3	0.3	—	0.8
India	—[c]	—	0.5	0.5	—	—[c]	1.0
Japan[a]	2.8	—	1.8	0.6	0.8	—	5.8
Africa and Middle East							
Israel[a]	4.4	—	—	2.2	0.6	0.3	7.7
Tunisia	0.4	1.6	2.0	1.7	—[c]	—	5.7
Turkey	0.4	—	0.7	0.2	—[c]	—	1.3
Union of South Africa[a]	1.4	0.1	0.6	1.8	—[c]	0.5	4.5

[a]Data relate to the fiscal year 1956-57.

[b]Administrative expenses are not included.

[c]Less than 0.05.

[d]Individual percentages may not add to totals because 1) of rounding errors, 2) administrative expenses that are not allocated to a particular program (or group of programs) are included in the total in some cases, and 3) transfers between programs are not included as a separate item.

Source: *The Cost of Social Security, 1949-1957* (Geneva, International Labour Office, 1961), pp. 28-190 and 205-10.

earnings than the earnings-related benefits paid in such countries as Belgium and West Germany.[6]

It might be expected that countries with highly developed social insurance programs would tend to spend comparatively little on public assistance, since public assistance systems in such countries are generally designed as supplementary programs —to provide for needy persons who for one reason or another are not eligible for social insurance benefits or whose benefits are inadequate. But among the ten top-ranking countries in relative social insurance expenditures, six were also among the ten top-ranking countries in the proportion of national income spent on public assistance. On the other hand, Portugal and Finland, which ranked highest in relative public assistance expenditures, had comparatively low social insurance expenditures, while New Zealand, whose social insurance expenditures were relatively high, spent only 0.1 percent of its national income on public assistance. Thus, generalizations on this particular relationship are hazardous, and, in fact, a great deal must be known about the relationship between social insurance programs and public assistance programs in each country before the statistical data can be properly interpreted. Even so, a population which provides political support for relatively liberal social insurance benefits will probably also tend to support reasonably adequate public assistance payments, and, in fact, where both types of systems exist side by side, there are both political and economic forces at work which tend to preserve a certain relationship between benefit levels under the two types of programs.

Although expenditures for veterans' benefits represent a larger proportion of total social security expenditures in the United States than in many other countries, they are not as large in relation to the national income as in a number of European countries.

[6]For some interesting comparisons, see 79. In 1959, the British amended their old-age insurance system to provide for supplementary earnings-related benefits which would augment the flat old-age benefits, but it will be some years before these supplements make an appreciable difference in the average level of benefits.

RELATIONSHIPS BETWEEN PUBLIC AND PRIVATE PROGRAMS

Although social security expenditures in the United States are not nearly as high in relation to national income as in many European and British countries, private employee benefit plans have grown rapidly and play an exceedingly important role in providing benefits that either supplement or, in the case of health insurance, take the place of social insurance benefits. The proportion of wage and salary workers covered by such plans in 1960 varied from 43 percent under pension or deferred profit-sharing plans to 74 percent under group life insurance plans.[7] Total employer and employee contributions to such plans amounted to an estimated $12.3 billion, or approximately 3 percent of the national income, in 1960.

In countries with more extensive and liberal social security programs, private employee benefit plans might be expected to play a relatively less important role. Unfortunately, such comparative data as are readily available are quite limited and not particularly recent (see Table 6). Unsatisfactory as the data are, they suggest that there may be a rough tendency toward an inverse relationship, among industrialized countries, between expenditures on statutory social security schemes and contributions to nonstatutory schemes expressed as a percentage of national income.[8] Further evidence of such a relationship is provided by an ILO study of labor costs in selected industries in ten European countries in 1955. In countries in which obligatory social security contributions by employers represented a particularly large percentage of total labor costs—Austria, Belgium, France,

[7] Actually, the smallest proportion of covered workers (3.4 percent) was found in the case of supplementary unemployment benefit plans, which are limited to a relatively small number of industries (200).

[8] However, such factors as differences in the size distribution and industrial composition of firms undoubtedly also play a role, since large firms and firms in certain industries are particularly likely to have employee benefit plans, and there is some evidence that the patterns of variation may be somewhat similar from country to country. A British study of private pension plans, for example, showed variations by size of firm and industry group that were quite similar to those revealed by American data (184, 209).

Table 6

CONTRIBUTIONS TO NONSTATUTORY SOCIAL SECURITY
SCHEMES, AS PERCENT OF NATIONAL INCOME, SELECTED
COUNTRIES, 1950-54

Country	1950	1951	1952	1953	1954
Australia			1.1[a]		
Canada			1.4	1.6	
West Germany					0.9
Sweden	0.9	1.0	1.1	1.1	1.1
Switzerland	1.2	1.3	1.0	1.1	1.1
United Kingdom				1.8	
United States					2.3

[a]Data apply to 1951-52.

*Sources: "Costs of Non-Statutory Social Security Schemes," *International Labour Review*, LXXVIII (October, 1958), 388-403, and *Statistical Yearbook* (United Nations, annual).

Greece, and Italy—employer contributions to nonobligatory social security schemes were very small or negligible as compared with those in Denmark, West Germany, and the United Kingdom, where obligatory employer contributions represented a smaller proportion of labor costs (175). This suggests that a high degree of employer resistance to contributions to private employee benefit schemes may be expected where employers are already contributing heavily to government schemes. Employer contributions to obligatory schemes were also a large proportion of total labor costs in Yugoslavia, but there were no contributions to nonobligatory schemes. Turkey, the tenth country, was a special case, since both obligatory and nonobligatory schemes were relatively undeveloped.

The whole question of the effect of fringe benefits on relative labor costs in European countries has been of special interest in relation to the probable effects of tariff reductions in the Common Market and Outer Seven areas (201).

It should also be noted that even though contributions to employee benefit plans appear to be relatively larger in relation to the national income in the United States than in the other countries represented in Table 6, combined costs of social security expenditures and contributions to private employee benefit plans would still appear to have been appreciably lower in the first half of the 1950s in the United States than in the other six countries, and this would undoubtedly also be true at present.

3. WELFARE PROGRAMS AND INCOME REDISTRIBUTION

Of basic importance to analysis of the economic effects of welfare programs is an understanding of the nature and extent of income redistribution which they bring about. The net income redistribution effect of all government fiscal measures will depend, of course, on the impact of all public taxation and spending activities on the various income groups, but welfare programs are likely to play an important role in any vertical income redistribution that occurs, since, although the share of upper income groups in their costs is not particularly large, the share of the very lowest income groups in the benefits tends to be high. It is sometimes contended that public welfare programs achieve only horizontal, rather than vertical, income redistribution, since they are (after account is taken of tax shifting) financed largely by the wage-earning class for the benefit of the wage-earning class. This ignores the fact, however, that the beneficiaries tend to be at the lower end of the income scale *within* the wage-earning class (and its children) because they are retired, widowed, orphaned, or disabled, or because their earnings have been severely reduced by unemployment.[1] To the extent that vertical income redistribution occurs as a result of welfare programs, it tends to be largely from average workers to families whose capacity to participate in the labor force is, for some reason, impaired. Or, as it has sometimes been put, most of it occurs within the income group under about $5,000 (55). In countries with extensive family

[1]In the case of unemployment insurance beneficiaries, of course, the reduction in income is usually only temporary, and many of them normally receive average or even above-average incomes.

allowance systems, transfers from small to large families are also of considerable significance (25 and 44).

Most attempts to measure statistically the income-redistribution effects of public welfare programs have been based on data for a single year, although in some cases comparisons with earlier years or earlier studies have been attempted. International comparisons are severely hampered because of the differences in methods that have been used by investigators in different countries. Furthermore, probably because of the almost insuperable statistical problems involved, none of the empirical studies, so far as I know, has attempted to take account of the fact that many beneficiaries of welfare payments would otherwise be partly or wholly supported by relatives or other individuals. Thus, the real benefits of transfer payments flow in part to persons who would otherwise be supporting the beneficiaries rather than to the beneficiaries themselves.

Finally, it is one thing to measure the income-redistribution effects of welfare programs in a single year. It is quite another, either empirically or theoretically, to attempt to assess their longer-run effects on the distribution of income.

In a study of the income-redistribution effects of government policies in 1950, Conrad estimated that (after adjusting for presumed shifting of the employers' portion of the contributory taxes) nearly 80 percent of social insurance taxes in 1950 were paid by those with incomes under $5,000 (9, p. 204). Musgrave's more recent estimates indicate that 52.3 percent of social insurance taxes were paid by those with incomes under $5,000 in 1954 and 29.0 percent by those with incomes of $5,000 to $7,500. His data on effective tax rates by income bracket show that, whereas the tax system as a whole is somewhat progressive, effective social insurance tax rates are regressive over the income distribution as a whole and fairly uniform for tax brackets under $5,000 (see Table 7).[2] Since public welfare programs other than those of the social insurance type are financed through general

2However, Conrad's data (9) indicated that in 1950 the effective tax rate was considerably lower for the under-$1,000 class than for the

tax revenues, Musgrave's estimates also provide an indication of the way in which the financing of these programs affects income groups. The fact that the combined state and local tax structure is somewhat regressive, whereas the federal tax structure is progressive, will clearly be relevant, from an economic point of view, to decisions affecting the distribution of the financing of such programs, e.g., public assistance, between the federal government and other levels of government. It should also be noted that the marked increase in the relative importance of social insurance programs has tended to make for more regressive over-all financing of welfare programs, although this should not necessarily be interpreted as an argument against the social insurance approach.

Conrad's data provide an indication of the manner in which social security and relief payments affected total income by income group in 1950 (9, pp. 197, 199). More recent data from the

Money income class (in dollars)	Income (in billions of dollars)	Percent derived from social security and relief
Under 1,000	6.09	40.3
1,000-2,000	18.70	5.9
2,000-3,000	31.28	1.0
3,000-4,000	36.31	0.4
4,000-5,000	28.67	0.3
5,000-7,500	37.80	0.2
7,500 and over	53.34	—[a]

[a]Less than 0.05.

Survey of Consumer Finances indicate that the proportion of spending units receiving transfer payments (chiefly of a public welfare type) in 1959 ranged from 13 percent in the highest income quintile to 55 percent in the lowest income quintile (51, p. 16).

A recent study by Morgan and others (38) presents some interesting findings on income inequality in 1959. As might have

---

$1,000-2,000 class. It should be noted, also, that Musgrave (39) used somewhat different assumptions from Conrad with respect to the manner in which employer contributory taxes were shifted.

Table 7

ESTIMATED EFFECTIVE RATES OF TAX, AS PERCENT OF INCOME, SOCIAL INSURANCE
TAXES AND ALL OTHER TAXES, FEDERAL AND STATE, 1954

Level of government and type of tax	Spending-unit income brackets.							
	0-$2,000	$2,000-3,000	$3,000-4,000	$4,000-5,000	$5,000-7,500	$7,500-10,000	Over $10,000	Total
Federal taxes								
Social insurance	3.6	4.1	4.4	4.2	3.2	2.4	1.1	3.0
All other taxes	12.1	13.8	14.7	15.8	19.0	21.8	32.1	20.9
State and local taxes								
Social insurance	0.5	0.7	0.7	0.9	0.7	0.6	0.3	0.6
All other taxes	10.7	9.7	9.1	8.9	8.9	8.1	7.4	8.5
All levels of government								
Social insurance	4.1	4.8	5.1	5.1	3.9	3.1	1.4	3.5
All other taxes	22.8	23.5	23.8	24.7	27.4	29.9	39.5	29.4
All taxes	26.9	28.3	28.9	29.8	31.3	33.0	40.9	32.9

Source: R. A. Musgrave, "The Incidence of Tax Structure and Its Effects on Consumption," in *Federal Tax Policy for Economic Growth and Stability*, (Washington, D.C., Government Printing Office, 1955), p. 97, papers submitted by panelists, November 9, 1955, U.S. Congress, Joint Committee on the Economic Report.

been expected, income inequality was found to be more pronounced for adult units (consisting of an individual aged 18 or
more, his spouse if he is married, and his children under 18), than
for spending units (related persons who live together and pool
their incomes) or families (related persons who live together).
This reflects the fact that adult units are particularly likely to
live with related adult units when the income of one or both units
is low. The net effect of money and nonmoney transfers, federal
income tax payments, and allowances for home-grown food and
the imputed rent of home-owners was to reduce income inequality
for adult units, as measured by the Lorenz coefficient,[3] from
.485 to .402. Unfortunately for our purposes, the authors did not
separate public from private transfers in presenting their data,
but the effect of total regular money transfers was evidently
relatively more important in reducing income inequality among
adult units than the effect of the federal income tax, nonmoney
transfers, or the other factors included in the analysis. However,
among family units, the effect of income tax payments was relatively more pronounced (38, p. 315). This is scarcely surprising,
since low-income units, who received transfer income but paid no
income taxes, figured more prominently among the adult units.

It is extremely difficult to determine the impact of welfare
programs on secular changes in the distribution of income. As the
late Selma Goldsmith has shown, to the extent that a reduction in
the inequality of income distribution occurred between 1929 and
1954, the change was concentrated in the period preceding the
end of World War II and particularly during the war years themselves, when a narrowing of wage differentials was chiefly responsible (21). However, as Garvy (19) and Denison (10) have
pointed out, the failure of data on the size distribution of income
among family or spending units to show an increase in the share
of the lowest quintile in the postwar period is probably partly at-

---

[3]The Lorenz coefficient of inequality is computed in such a way
that it would equal zero if all units had the same incomes and unity if
one unit received all the income and the others received nothing. Thus,
the higher the coefficient, the greater is income inequality (38, pp.
310-11).

tributable to the fact that there has been an increase in the proportion of low-income families and individuals, particularly in
the aged population, who maintain separate households. Were it
not for this "undoubling," families and individuals in the lower
part of the income distribution would show a larger average increase in income.

A few of the industrial countries of western Europe, for
which data are available, have shown trends similar to those in
the United States, but the timing of changes has differed. As
Solow (50) has pointed out, there is evidence that in the United
Kingdom, The Netherlands, and Sweden the process of equalization continued past the end of the war. He also notes that in recent years the lowest quintile has had a noticeably smaller share
of total income in the United States than in the United Kingdom
or Sweden, but warns that detailed investigation would be required to determine whether this reflects differences in the extent of social security programs, or other factors.

As various writers have indicated, government provision of
certain public services, particularly public education, has probably had a more important effect on the relative real income position of the lower income groups than cash income-maintenance
payments (31). Brittain (2) maintains that there was a substantial
reduction in income inequality in Great Britain between 1938 and
1949 as a result of the impact of fiscal policy and social services (including the imputed value of food subsidies, education,
health, and housing expenditures), but a slight increase in inequality from 1949 to 1955. However, the fact that the wartime
food subsidies disappeared in the early 1950s must be kept in
mind in interpreting this finding. The influence of the decline in
the unemployment rate must also be recognized, not only in interpreting changes in the early 1950s in Great Britain, but also
in connection with all comparisons of income redistribution in
the postwar period and in the 1930s.[4] A Danish study (33) indicated that "equalization by way of social expenditure" in Den-

---

[4]On income redistribution in Great Britain, see also 5. For another
very recent study of income distribution, see 52.

mark appeared to be less important in 1949 than in 1938-39. The main explanation was the more favorable employment situation in 1949, which meant that income-maintenance payments to the unemployed were playing a relatively smaller role.

In the long run, as Lampman (31) has argued, the most important factor making for reduction in income inequality is probably the shift into higher paid occupations and industries. And yet, to the extent that welfare programs affect the growth of aggregate demand, on the one hand, and the quality of the labor supply, on the other, they may have a significant effect on these long-run changes in the occupational and industrial distribution of the labor force.

4. THE OLD-AGE, SURVIVORS, AND DISABILITY INSURANCE PROGRAM

Dwarfing all other American public welfare programs in total expenditures and in the number of persons affected is the federal Old-Age, Survivors, and Disability Insurance program. Established under the provisions of the Social Security Act of 1935, the program has been greatly expanded and liberalized through numerous amendments adopted during the last quarter-century. It is the only social insurance program financed and administered entirely by the federal government.[1] By 1960, total OASDI expenditures were about $11 billion. On the basis of revised estimates made after adoption of the 1961 amendments, expenditures were expected to reach $18 billion by 1970 (see Table 8).

A very large proportion of the writing by professional economists on OASDI, and perhaps a disproportionate amount, has been concerned with financing issues, particularly with the question of the extent to which a reserve should be accumulated. This issue, though understandably of great concern in the early stages of the program, is less vital now that revenues and expenditures tend to be quite similar in amount. Meanwhile, other issues of considerable significance for the economy have been neglected.

LABOR FORCE PARTICIPATION AND PRODUCTIVITY

There is some evidence that the OASDI program has encouraged withdrawal from the labor force, as well as a greater tendency to work on a part-time basis. These effects can be most

[1]Rehabilitation of persons who are eligible for disability insurance, however, is administered by the states.

Table 8

STATUS OF THE OLD-AGE, SURVIVORS, AND DISABILITY INSURANCE TRUST FUNDS (CONSOLIDATED), ACTUAL DATA, 1937–60, AND ESTIMATES OF FUTURE OPERATIONS UNDER THE 1961 AMENDMENTS

(High-employment assumptions based on intermediate-cost estimates at 3.02 percent interest; in millions of dollars)

Calendar year	Contributions [a]	Benefit payments	Administrative expenses	Railroad retirement financial interchange	Interest on fund	Balance in fund
Actual data						
1937	765	1	–		2	766
1940	325	35	26		43	2,031
1945	1,285	274	30		134	7,121
1950	2,671	961	61		257	13,721
1951	3,367	1,885	81		417	15,540
1952	3,819	2,194	88		365	17,442
1953	3,945	3,006	88		414	18,707
1954	5,163	3,670	92		468	20,576
1955	5,713	4,968	119		461	21,663
1956	6,172	5,715	132		531	22,519
1957	6,825	7,347	162		557	22,393
1958	7,566	8,327	194	– 121	549	21,864
1959	8,052	9,842	184	– 275	525	20,141
1960	10,866	10,677	203	– 308	506	20,324

Estimated data (short-range estimate)					
1961	12,757	12,825	311	− 310	570	22,495
1962	13,455	14,180	308	− 305	580	21,737
1963	15,746	14,928	310	− 325	601	22,521
1964	16,623	15,557	325	− 320	649	23,591
1965	17,035	16,073	339	− 305	708	24,617
Estimated data (long-range estimate)					
1970	21,769	18,174	298	− 160	1,364	43,418
1975	23,573	21,109	318	− 91	1,880	64,351
1980	25,372	24,238	332	1	2,386	81,784
2000	34,238	33,573	436	86	4,030	137,779
2020	41,648	45,897	559	86	7,739	261,918

[a]Includes reimbursement for additional cost of noncontributory credit for military service.

Sources: *Social Security Bulletin: Annual Statistical Supplement* (1960), 19, and R. J. Myers, "Old-Age, Survivors, and Disability Insurance: Financing Basis and Policy Under the 1961 Amendments," *Social Security Bulletin*, XXIV (September, 1961), 17.

readily analyzed with respect to elderly men, but other groups of beneficiaries have also been affected. However, the influence of OASDI cannot be neatly separated from the effects of public assistance and private pensions.

In his voluminous study of labor force changes, Long (181, p. 163) concluded that "social security and pensions were far from being the main force (though they doubtless helped) in bringing about the withdrawal of elderly persons from the labor market."[2] Gertrude Bancroft (142, pp. 136-37) seems to attach somewhat greater weight to OASDI, maintaining that "the age group 65 and over has been showing declining rates of labor force activity in almost every decade, and this decline appears to gather some momentum with each extension of Social Security coverage or liberalization of benefits."[3]

Long's analysis relied heavily on an attempt to determine whether there was a relationship between decade-to-decade changes in labor force participation rates and other types of changes. The difficulty with this approach is that changes in labor force participation rates over any given period will have been influenced by a number of forces, some of which may have exerted their influence in opposite directions. In World War II, for example, old-age insurance benefits were being paid out for the first time, but the labor market was exceedingly tight, and the labor force participation rate of elderly men rose appreciably in response to favorable employment opportunities.

[2]He also held (181, p. 173) that "the reduction in the proportion of older men in the labor force was closely connected with both the level and change of employment." They left the labor force in large numbers "during 1890-1910 and 1930-34, when there were almost no government assistance and private pension plans, and still more dropped out between 1930 and 1940, although old-age assistance (charity payments) was inadequate during that decade and was not effectively supplemented by social security until after 1940" (181, p. 163).

[3]Furthermore, commenting on the decline in labor force participation rates of nonwhite women, she indicates that "where other sources of support were available—such as husband's earnings, or pension or other types of Social Security payments for needy and dependent persons—nonwhite women tended to reduce their labor force activity, particularly in the age groups where young children at home are a determining factor" (142, p. 55). See also 143.

However, over the entire period from 1930 to 1960, the labor-force participation rate of elderly men fell much more sharply than in the preceding 30-year period (see Table 9). This is not to suggest that social security programs were wholly responsible —depression in the thirties, increased unemployment in the late fifties, occupational and industrial changes, the growth of pension and of compulsory retirement systems, and a generally rising income level probably played a role (111).

For closer analysis of the role of income-maintenance programs in accelerating the rate of retirement, there is a need for studies which consider the *relationship* between prospective retirement income and income before retirement. The Cornell retirement study (132 and 133) moved a step in this direction by analyzing the influence of both current income and prospective retirement income on the attitudes of men who were approaching retirement. It was found that favorable attitudes toward retirement were positively correlated with anticipated retirement income, but that current income per se did not have a significant influence on attitudes toward retirement except insofar as it was related to anticipated retirement income.

But does a prospective retirement income of $3,000 a year appear equally attractive to a skilled craftsman who has been earning $6,000 a year and a corporation executive with a $100,000 salary? If, as seems more reasonable, it is the ratio of retirement income to income while employed that is important, we might expect to find that in countries in which benefits available under a national old-age insurance or pension scheme are high in relation to average earnings a relatively small proportion of elderly men would be in the labor force. Investigating this relationship for 14 industrialized countries around 1950, I found a significantly high inverse correlation (−.83) between the proportion of men aged 65 and over in the labor force and average benefits under the national old-age insurance or pension system expressed as a percentage of average annual earnings in the country (109).[4]

[4] A somewhat lower, but nevertheless significant, correlation (-.66) was found between the proportion of elderly men in the labor force and average old-age benefits expressed as a percentage of national per capita income.

Table 9

PERCENTAGE OF PERSONS IN THE LABOR FORCE BY AGE AND SEX, UNITED STATES, SELECTED YEARS, 1890–1960

Age (in years)	Men							Women						
	1890	*1900*	*1920*	*1930*	*1940*	*1950*	*1960*	*1890*	*1900*	*1920*	*1930*	*1940*	*1950*	*1960*
Total	84.3	85.7	84.6	82.1	79.7	79.4	77.4	18.2	20.0	22.7	23.6	25.7	29.3	34.5
14–19	50.0[a]	62.1[a]	51.5	40.1	35.4	39.9	26.5	24.5[a]	26.8[a]	28.4	22.8	19.0	23.0	14.0
20–24	90.9	90.6	89.9	88.8	88.4	82.5	80.1	30.2	31.7[a]	37.5	41.8	45.6	43.6	45.3
25–34	96.0	94.9	96.3	96.0	95.8	92.8	94.9	16.8	19.4	23.7	27.1	33.3	32.0	35.3
35–44	95.9	94.5	95.4	95.7	95.4	95.2	95.6	12.7	15.0	19.2	21.7	27.3	35.2	42.7
45–54	93.9	92.8	93.4	93.8	92.7	92.5 }	89.0	12.5	14.2	17.9	19.7	22.4	33.1 }	41.6
55–64	89.0	86.2	86.3	86.5	84.5	83.9 }		11.4	12.6	14.3	15.3	16.6	23.6 }	
65 and over	68.3	63.1	55.6	53.9	42.2	41.5	30.5	7.6	8.3	7.3	7.3	6.0	7.9	10.3

[a]Percentages based on small numbers.

Sources: Gertrude Bancroft, *The American Labor Force* (New York, John Wiley and Sons, Inc., 1958), p. 207, and *U.S. Census of Population, 1960: United States Summary, General Social and Economic Characteristics* (Washington, D.C., Government Printing Office, 1962), Table 84, U.S. Bureau of the Census, PC(1)1C.

Income, of course, exerts its influence in conjunction with other factors that have a significant impact on the propensity to retire, including health status, occupation, compulsory retirement provisions, the state of the labor market, and personality differences. Of these, compulsory retirement is less important than is commonly assumed, while health status is of overriding importance. Large-scale studies conducted on both sides of the Atlantic in the early 1950s (125, 128, and 129) indicated that when retired persons were asked about their reasons for retirement a large proportion replied that they had retired voluntarily because of ill health. Only a relatively small minority indicated that they had retired because of compulsory retirement systems or other types of involuntary separations from their jobs.[5] Furthermore, some of those who were compelled to retire later returned to work, usually in some type of part-time employment, whereas those who retired because of ill health were less likely to return to work. Thus, the retired population reflects the net effect of a sifting-out process, which tends to leave those who are suffering from some type of physical or mental disability in the permanently retired group.

Does the decline in labor force participation of elderly men, as well as their increasing propensity to work part-time, mean that the real national product is suffering because the nation is deprived of the services of elderly men who in earlier periods would have been more likely to work full time? The late Sumner Slichter (126) and others have argued vigorously that the loss of GNP is sizable.

This argument clearly carries more weight in a period of tight labor market conditions than in a period of substantial unemployment. It would also be more convincing if compulsory re-

---

[5]It should be noted that other types of studies—based on samples of retirees from large firms, where compulsory retirement systems are prevalent—have indicated that a majority of the respondents retired because of a mandatory retirement system, but these results were clearly influenced by the specialized nature of the sample.

tirement systems were actually the chief factor responsible for retirement. Although there is reason to believe that compulsory retirement systems have become more prevalent in the last decade, along with the growth of private pension plans, only a minority of workers are affected by them. The great majority of elderly persons who are out of the labor force do not consider themselves well enough to work, or, in the case of women, have had no work experience since before age 50 (129, Chaps. IV and V).[6]

Thus, although there is no clear evidence of a *general tendency* for productivity to decline with advancing age among employed workers (104 and 137), it is highly likely that the productivity of elderly persons who are out of the labor force is, on the average, substantially lower than that of employed workers. Historically, moreover, the decline in the proportion of elderly men in the labor force (and also of teenagers) has been accompanied by a marked increase in the labor force participation of women. And, as Long (181, p. 24) has pointed out, there is considerable evidence "that women displaced elderly men because of their better training for many clerical, personal service, and professional jobs in comparison to their relative wages." The fact that older persons tend to have had less schooling than younger persons is well known. Perhaps less appreciated is the fact that the difference has been widening.[7]

[6]More recent data (116)—based on interviews with a nationwide sample conducted by the Survey Research Center of the University of Michigan in 1960—indicated that nearly half of the heads of spending units aged 65 and over reported that they had some physical, mental, or nervous conditions which limited their ability to work. The proportion would undoubtedly be higher among the retired than the nonretired. The data also indicated that about a fifth of the wives of spending unit heads and a quarter of the dependent adults in the 65 and older age bracket were disabled.

[7]The ratio of years of school completed by elderly men to those completed by young men and women declined from nearly eight-tenths in 1910 to scarcely more than four tenths in 1950 (181, p. 14). There is reason to believe, however, that the difference will begin to narrow in the next few decades (110).

Looked at from this point of view, the displacement of elderly men by younger men and women may be viewed as one of the ways in which adaptation to economic change and higher productivity are achieved.[8] Yet this should not be construed as an argument in favor of policies requiring retirement at an arbitrary age.

If we accept the point of view that a program like OASDI—provided its detailed features are appropriately framed—can have positive effects on the conservation of human resources and on productivity, are there modifications in its provisions that should be considered to make it more effective in this respect? Should we, for example, consider paying child's benefits to age 21, or perhaps even to age 25, as in some European social security programs, if the young person is pursuing higher education or training? Should we take steps to make the rehabilitation provisions of the disability insurance program more effective and also expand the program to apply to severe permanent partial disability, as most European "invalidity insurance" programs do? Should we proceed to substantial further liberalization or elimination of the retirement test, or, in view of the costs involved, should higher priority be given to improving benefits, particularly in view of the needs of the large numbers of beneficiaries who are too old or disabled to work (98, 100, 102, 118, and 134)?

From a long-run point of view, moreover, a most important question concerns the future development of policy with respect to the age of retirement. Concern over unemployment is currently creating pressure for earlier retirement. But as life expectancy gradually increases, even for those who have already reached their sixties, should OASDI policy be revised to encourage later retirement? And should this be done through raising the age of eligibility or by creating a kind of "retirement zone" in which actuarially reduced benefits might continue to be available at age 62, as at present, normal benefits at age 65, and perhaps

---

[8]For an estimate of the effect of changes in the age-sex composition of employment and the increase in the relative contribution of women workers on the rate of economic growth from 1929 to 1957, see 11.

special credits be made available for those postponing retirement
until after age 65?[9]

THE INCOME STATUS OF THE AGED

Since earners in the aged population typically have considerably more income than nonearners (129, Chap. VIII), the decline in the labor force participation of elderly men has exerted
downward pressure on the average income position of the aged,
even while increases in OASDI benefits and in benefits available under private pension plans and public employee retirement
systems have been making possible higher average money incomes
in retirement.

Between 1948 and 1960 the increase in the number and proportion of elderly persons receiving income from OASDI was
striking (see Table 10). By 1960, 64 percent of all those aged 65
and over were receiving old-age benefits under the program. The
proportions receiving income from other public retirement systems
and from veterans' programs had also increased appreciably,
while the percentage receiving earnings had declined, as had the
proportion receiving public assistance. Highly significant, also,
was the marked decline in the proportion receiving no money income or income solely from other sources (e.g., private pensions).

Despite these trends, studies that have attempted to ap-
praise the adequacy of the incomes of the elderly have indicated
that the problem of poverty in old age has by no means disappeared. The most intensive study of this type is based on data
that are now more than ten years old, but its methods and findings are worth mentioning. Recognizing that neither the personal
income nor the family income data available from census surveys

---

[9]The objection is frequently raised that if credits for postponed retirement are based on actuarial estimates of the savings to the system
from postponement of retirement they will be too small to have much
effect. This seems especially likely if we accept the view that it is the
ratio between expected retirement income and income before retirement
that is important. For further discussion of this point, see 111, p. 33.
See, also, 91. None of these papers discusses, however, the impact of
such provisions on retirement policies in private industry, which needs
to be taken into account.

were well adapted to analysis of the income status of the aged—
since the former obscured the extent to which husbands and
wives pooled their income while the latter obscured the income
status of elderly persons who were living with relatives—Steiner
and Dorfman (129, Chap. VIII) set out to develop data on the income status of elderly "economic units"—couples, unrelated
males, and unrelated females. Their findings, which were based
on a special nationwide follow-up survey of persons aged 65 and
over conducted by the U. S. Bureau of the Census in the spring
of 1952, indicated that about 44 percent of the couples, 50 percent of the unrelated males, and 69 percent of the unrelated
females had cash receipts in 1951 that fell below estimated
budgetary requirements for a "modest, but adequate" level of
living as defined by the U. S. Bureau of Labor Statistics.[10] Even
more striking were the indications that more than a quarter of the

Table 10

ESTIMATED NUMBER OF PERSONS AGED 65 AND OVER
RECEIVING MONEY INCOME FROM SPECIFIED SOURCES,[a]
UNITED STATES, JUNE, 1948 AND DECEMBER, 1960

| | *June, 1948* | | *December, 1960* | |
| | Number in | | Number in | |
Source of money income[b]	*thousands*	*Percent*	*thousands*	*Percent*
Total, aged 65 and over	11,540	100.0	16,960	100.0
Employment	3,830	33.2	4,110	24.2
Earners	2,930	25.4	3,220	19.0
Earners' wives not themselves employed	900	7.8	890	5.2
Social insurance and related programs[c]	2,330	20.2	12,010	70.8
Old-age, survivors, and disability insurance	1,460	12.7	10,820	63.7
Railroad retirement insurance	300	2.6	650	3.8
Government employees' retirement programs	300	2.6	1,020	6.0

[10]It should be noted that some of the wives were less than 65
years of age.

Table 10 (Continued)

Source of money income[b]	June, 1948 Number in thousands	Percent	December, 1960 Number in thousands	Percent
Veterans' compensation and pension programs	350	3.0	1,670	9.8
Public assistance[d]	2,400	20.8	2,410	14.2
No money income or income solely from other sources	3,400	29.4	1,490	8.4
Income from more than one of specified sources	420	3.6	n.a.	n.a.
Employment and social insurance or assistance	270	2.3	n.a.	n.a.
Social insurance and public assistance	150	1.3	740	4.4

[a]Data for 1960 for the continental United States, Alaska, Hawaii, Puerto Rico, and the Virgin Islands; 1948 data for the continental United States. Persons with incomes from sources specified may also have received money income from other sources, such as interest, dividends, private pensions or annuities, or cash contributions from relatives.

[b]The sum of the persons shown under the four categories exceeds the number in the population by the estimated number with income from more than one of the three main sources. The estimates of persons with income from more than one source, developed from survey data, are subject to sampling variability (which may be relatively large for the smaller estimates) and to such errors as may result from attempts to adjust for developments since the sample surveys were conducted.

[c]Persons with income from more than one of the programs listed are counted only once. Unemployment insurance, workmen's compensation, and temporary disability insurance programs also provide income for some aged persons, but information is lacking as to the numbers.

[d]Old-age assistance recipients and persons aged 65 and over receiving aid to the blind or to the permanently and totally disabled; includes a small number receiving vendor payments for medical care but no direct cash payment.

Sources: Lenore A. Epstein, "Money Income of Aged Persons: A 10-Year Review, 1948 to 1958," Social Security Bulletin, XXII (June, 1959), 4, and "The Aged in the Population and Their Income Sources," Social Security Bulletin, XXIV (July, 1961), 7.

couples, about a third of the unrelated males, and approximately half of the unrelated females did not have enough receipts for a bare subsistence level of living.

More recent data based on a special survey conducted by the Survey Research Center of the University of Michigan in the spring of 1960 have been reported by Morgan and David (116, p. 192). Using a "standard" budget developed for administration of assistance to needy elderly couples and individuals in New York City, they found that 43 percent of the spending units in the nation headed by a man aged 65 or older and 70 percent of those headed by a female aged 65 or more did not have enough gross disposable income in 1959 to meet such a standard. Similar indications of a substantial amount of poverty among elderly couples and individuals in Great Britain may be found in a preliminary report on a survey conducted by the Department of Applied Economics of Cambridge University in 1959-60 (101).[11]

INCOME-REDISTRIBUTION EFFECTS

OASDI effects transfers of income from the average income-receiver to families suffering from the loss or severe disablement of the chief breadwinner and to the aged. It is possible to develop estimates of the impact of OASDI taxes and benefits by income level, but unless such estimates go beyond the primary effects of the initial transfers and take account of the secondary effects, they are of limited usefulness. Furthermore, it must be recognized that if the OASDI program did not exist the beneficiaries would probably be receiving income from some combination of other sources—earnings, public assistance, or relatives' contributions—to a greater extent than at present. Some guesses can be made as to the types of adjustment required by these considerations, but it is impossible to estimate, for example, how many people would be on public assistance and what average

[11]A particularly interesting finding was that a quarter of the economic units in the survey were receiving national assistance, while about 27 percent had incomes below the budgetary standards set by the Assistance Board but were not receiving assistance payments. Like the Steiner-Dorfman study, the Cole study indicated that elderly widows constituted by far the most impoverished group in the aged population.

monthly assistance payments would be today if there were no
such thing as OASDI.

Carroll's recent study provides estimates of the income-
redistribution effects of OASDI, without, however, attempting to
take account of any of the complications that have just been
mentioned (94). His data suggest that in 1958 there was a net
transfer of some $4.5 billion from expenditure units with incomes
(including transfer income) of $3,000 or more to those with in-
comes of less than $3,000. The largest net gain, amounting to
about $2.5 billion, accrued to spending units in the $1,000-1,999
income class. All told, the shifting was primarily from the average income receivers—those with incomes of $3,000 to $7,499,
who experienced a net loss of about $2.5 billion—to the low in-
come groups.

But, as we have previously suggested, OASDI transfers indirectly benefit—to some immeasurable extent—the relatives who
would otherwise be supporting OASDI beneficiaries and the
families of those persons, particularly middle-aged married
women, whose entry into the labor force has been indirectly facilitated by the withdrawal of elderly and disabled men and by the
nonparticipation of young widows in the labor force. On the
whole, it appears likely that the families who benefit are chiefly
in the lower-middle income groups. On the other hand, the upper
income groups are probably contributing substantially less to
OASDI than they would be to public assistance if there were no
OASDI program. All these considerations suggest that, on net
balance, the transfers effected by OASDI are primarily from
middle-income receivers to lower and lower-middle income groups.

CONSUMPTION, SAVING, AND INVESTMENT

The effects of OASDI on economic stability and economic
growth will depend to a considerable extent on its short-run and
long-run effects on consumption, saving, and investment. An old-
age insurance system, based at least partly on reserve financing,
is likely to have a restrictive effect on consumption and a deflationary effect on the economy during its early stages, when con-

tributions substantially exceed benefits. It was this prospect that disturbed economists during the 1930s (65).[12] As it turned out, OASDI largely went through this stage from 1937 to 1956, a period which for the most part was dominated by inflationary tendencies. Thus, the deflationary impact of OASDI probably operated as a restraint on the generally inflationary trends in the economy.

Does it follow that OASDI is likely to have a neutral effect on aggregate consumption when contributions and expenditures are approximately in balance? Not necessarily. It is entirely possible that the income transfers effected through OASDI may have a stimulating effect on consumption when contributions and expenditures are approximately in balance and even when the former slightly exceed the latter. This possibility rests on the proposition, emphasized by Keynes in the *General Theory* (27, Chaps. 8-10), but influenced to a considerable extent by consumption theories developed by earlier economists, that transfers of income from higher to lower income groups will tend to increase aggregate consumption because lower income groups are likely to spend a larger fraction of increments of income (in the economists' terms, the marginal propensity to consume is inversely related to level of family income). Furthermore, the primary effect on consumption may be augmented by a secondary effect if the initial increase in consumption stimulates a further increase in income and consumption through the multiplier (26).

However, several articles published in the late forties cast serious doubt on the size of the consumption changes that would be stimulated by income redistribution (34 and 41). Their results reflect the fact that the possibilities of achieving substantial redistribution of income are limited because the bulk of taxable income is in the middle and lower income groups. Furthermore, although the *average* propensity to consume shows a marked inverse relationship with income, variations in the *marginal* propensity to consume by income group are much less pronounced, particularly when account is taken of the dissaving by lower in-

[12]For more recent discussions, see 45, 48, and 64.

come groups which consistently shows up in survey data. (To the extent that increments of income received by lower income spending units through redistributional measures merely replace dissaving, they will not necessarily increase consumption.)

However, neglect of the multiplier effects of the initial increase in consumption represented an important limitation on these findings. In a 1955 article, Bronfenbrenner, Yamane, and Lee (3) pointed out that the percentage increases in consumption estimated by Lubell (for income-redistribution policies of varying extent) should be multiplied by about three, to take account of the multiplier effects of the shift in the aggregate consumption function. In an article published at the same time, Conrad (8) showed that when the secondary effects of income redistribution (as affected by public budgets in the United States in 1950) are taken into account, there is a substantial effect on consumption, but the amount of income redistribution affected is less than would appear to occur if only the initial impact is considered.

Various writers have suggested that the marginal propensity to consume may be much higher among recipients of public welfare payments than among other spending units with low incomes. Pursuing this line of reasoning, and building on earlier work by the U. S. Social Security Board (75), Carroll (94) has developed (along with his estimates of the income-redistribution effects of OASDI, discussed earlier) estimates of the effects of OASDI on consumption based on existing estimates of the marginal propensity to consume by income class *and* on the special assumption that the marginal propensity to consume of beneficiary spending units with incomes below $4,000 is .95, as compared with a marginal propensity of .78 for all spending units in this income bracket. [13] His computations indicate that, on these assumptions, $317 million was added to consumption through transfers to OASDI beneficiaries in 1956 and about a billion dollars in 1958. Although these estimates are of interest, they take no account of indirect effects.

[13]The choice of a marginal propensity of .95, rather than 1.00, is designed to allow for the fact that a moderate amount of dissaving can be expected among beneficiary units.

This type of approach, moreover, would be thrown into question by the Duesenberry (12) hypothesis, which holds that consumption is a function of previous peak income, and by the newer theories of Modigliani (37) and Friedman (17), which treat consumption as a function of expected lifetime income (16). Although these theories differ in detail, they all suggest that "households whose income is above the level to which they are adjusted save an abnormally large proportion and those whose income is below this level save an abnormally low proportion, or even dissave" (37, p. 418). A growing population will, in general, mean a relatively small number of retired people, and hence of dissavers. Furthermore, an upward trend in real income per head will mean that the savers will, on the average, have larger lifetime incomes than the dissavers. Thus, on certain relatively simplified assumptions, the savings ratio will tend to be proportional to the rate of growth of aggregate real disposable income (15, p. 685). This proposition has extremely important implications for theories of economic growth.

The newer theories also imply that population groups with comparatively stable incomes will be more likely than those with unstable incomes to increase their consumption proportionately with increases in current income (their income elasticity of consumption will be close to unity), since changes in their current incomes will be likely to be highly correlated with changes in their normal incomes.

These theories have a good many implications for the analysis of welfare policies, which have not been fully worked out. Traditional analysis, which is based on the principle that the marginal propensity to consume is inversely related to current income level, implies, as we have seen, that in the short run transfers from higher to lower income groups will stimulate consumption, while the long-run effects of welfare programs will depend to a considerable extent on whether or not they lead to a permanent shift in the household consumption function. Possibly the stability of the savings ratio in the United States since the closing decades of the nineteenth century (20, Vol. I, Chap. I; and 29, pp. 52-54), in the *face* of a rise in real income which would have been expected to result in an increase in the savings ratio, can be explained on the assumption that there has been an upward shift in the household consumption function (22, pp. 98-107), and some would argue that this might be at least partially attributable to social security.[14]

On the basis of the newer theories, however, long-run stability in the savings ratio may reasonably be expected, without the need to assume that any shift in consumption or saving habits has occurred. According to Modigliani (37), transfers from higher to lower income groups need not have important short-run effects on consumption, since consumption is not regarded as a stable function of current income, the transfer payments go in large part to persons who would otherwise presumably be dissaving, and in any event the proportion of personal income saved is determined in large part by the rate of change of aggregate real income.

It must be recognized, however, that, although dissaving occurs on a considerable scale among the short-term unemployed, there is evidence that it takes place only on a very limited scale among the aged. The Steiner-Dorfman study (129, pp. 115-19) indicated that dissaving accounted for only 6 to 8 percent of total receipts of the aged in 1951 (when the proportion of elderly persons receiving OASDI benefits was much smaller than it is today) and that it played an important role only for a small proportion of the aged. Data from the *Survey of Consumer Finances* (51, p. 80), moreover, indicate that relatively few spending units approach old age with assets large enough to provide a basis for appreciable dissaving over an extended period of retirement.

[14]Kuznets indicates, in his recent volume on capital formation (28, pp. 454-56), that the personal savings ratio was slightly lower in 1948-57 than in 1939-41, and that rather low ratios of personal savings to personal and disposable income may be expected in the future because 1) patterns of social behavior will encourage higher consumption, 2) technological change will create new products which consumers will want, 3) full employment policies, progressive taxation, and to some extent rising prices have made for less unequal distribution of disposable income, and 4) if international tensions continue, savings may be discouraged because of a continued sense of insecurity about the future.

Among spending units aged 55 to 64, for example, 63 percent had liquid assets of less than $2,000 in 1960.

Welfare expenditures might be expected to induce a shift in the consumption function to the extent that they resulted in greater *stability* of income. Pursuing this line of reasoning, Friedman (17, pp. 56-58) has pointed out that the higher average propensities to consume (at comparable income levels) in Great Britain than in the United States might be at least partly explained by Britain's more extensive social security system. [15] A more detailed comparison of British and American data by Lansing and Lydall (32) suggests that the lower personal saving ratio in Britain can be explained chiefly by two factors: 1) a higher wealth-income ratio in Britain, carried over from before the war and only gradually eliminated, and 2) the influence of differences in structural characteristics of the two populations, particularly the smaller proportions of self-employed persons and home-owners and the larger proportion of retired persons in Britain. However, their data on the ratio of holdings of liquid assets to disposable personal income (used as an approximation for the wealth-income ratio) show that the British ratio exceeded the United States ratio in the immediate postwar period but fell much more sharply and by 1958 was below the American ratio. Could this mean that the British, with their more extensive social security protection, find it less necessary to hold liquid assets than formerly? Here it should be noted that probably the most significant difference between the prewar and postwar situations was effected by the introduction of the National Health Service, which is not a welfare program in our special sense, but which does, of course, provide substantial protection against the contingency of heavy medical expenses.

[15]Friedman also called attention to the higher average propensity to consume (for comparable levels of income) in Sweden, but did not attempt detailed comparisons between Sweden and the other two countries because of certain technical differences in the Swedish data. It should be noted that higher average propensities to consume in Britain and Sweden do not necessarily mean that the proportion of aggregate income saved is smaller, since a substantial amount of saving is done by business firms and public agencies.

Thus far, we have been considering the effects of social security programs in general, rather than the particular effects of a long-term insurance program like OASDI. Unfortunately, it is extremely difficult to disentangle the effects of OASDI from those of other factors, either on the basis of historical or cross-sectional data.

Cross-sectional data, for example, do not permit us to compare the saving and spending habits of persons covered by OASDI with those who are not, since nearly everyone is covered by OASDI or some other public retirement program. However, there is evidence that at each income level persons who are contributing to private pension funds in both Britain and the United States save more in a given year than those who are not contributing (32).[16] From this it could be inferred that OASDI might also have similar effects on individual saving, but private pension plans might well result in a greater increase in aggregate saving, since they are currently accumulating far more than they are paying out from year to year. The detailed report on the study being conducted by the National Bureau of Economic Research, now nearing completion, should shed more light on these relationships (4).[17]

Even so, there would seem to be a need for a great deal more research on these questions. Is the evidence on the impact of pension plans on personal saving convincing, or are those who are covered by pension plans likely to save more because they tend to be more highly educated or differently distributed by oc-

[16]It should also be noted that total saving *less* pension fund payments for those who make such payments is about the same as total saving for those who do not make pension payments.

See, also, 36 for evidence that payments to pension and retirement funds do not tend to reduce the fraction of income devoted to life insurance. Similarly, in an article on the effects of the German pension reform of 1957 (113), it has been pointed out that the very substantial increase in the level of current and prospective pension benefits affected by the changes in the system did not have an adverse effect on either private insurance or savings.

[17]According to a preliminary report on the findings the study is reaching the conclusion that "the development of retirement programs has significantly enlarged the ratio of national saving...."

cupation from those who are not covered? If such evidence does prove to be reliable on the basis of further analysis, does it suggest that long-term social insurance programs have an effect on saving habits opposite from those of short-term programs?

Cross-sectional studies of family income and expenditure patterns, including, where feasible, international comparisons, would seem to offer promise of shedding more light on these relationships. Even more valuable are comparable cross-sectional data for different time periods or panel data which indicate how the income and expenditures of a constant sample of families change over time. It would be particularly interesting to gain greater insight into the relationship between increased social security expenditures and high rates of economic growth in postwar Europe. Coming at a time when other influences, such as Marshall Plan aid and postwar reconstruction, were encouraging both public and private investment, the stimulating effects of increased welfare expenditures on consumption may, when multiplier effects are taken into account, have played a significant role in a combination of economic developments that was highly favorable to the growth of consumption and investment. At present, all we are in a position to say is that the postwar experience of such countries as France and West Germany suggests that heavy social security expenditures are not incompatible with high rates of economic growth.

The newer developments in consumption theory also strongly suggest the need for less emphasis, in empirical research, on consumption and income relationships in a single year and much more emphasis on the ratio of consumption to income over longer periods (e.g., three years) and over the life cycle. In recent years there has been an encouraging shift in this direction. As a result of increased emphasis on analysis of income, consumption, and saving over the life cycle, economists may ultimately develop a more satisfactory interpretation of the effects of a program like OASDI.

CONSUMPTION PATTERNS

Engel's famous law (14), which held that the proportion of income spent on food tended to decline with increasing income, represented one of the first attempts to formulate a theory of the influence of income on the distribution of consumption expenditures . This theory, as well as later work on the income elasticity of consumption, would imply that transfers of income to lower income groups would tend to increase the consumption of staples at the expense of luxury goods. Here again, however, we must keep in mind the fact that in the absence of OASDI and other public welfare programs many of the beneficiaries would be receiving support from other sources, particularly earnings and relatives' contributions.

Thus, although data on variations in consumption patterns by income level, family size, and age of family head (107) are essential in the estimation of the budgetary requirements of beneficiaries, they can be highly misleading if used as the sole basis for estimating the impact of a program such as OASDI on the demand for particular goods and services. It seems likely, for example, that the requirements of OASDI beneficiaries for staple food items would, for the most part, be met in the absence of such a program. Many of those, however, whose earning capacity is impaired and who would otherwise be dependent on relatives, probably spend more on apparel and personal services than they would in the absence of OASDI benefits. The implications for expenditures on medical care are difficult to analyze (because medical expenses are met from a variety of sources), although it seems likely that if Congress should enact legislation providing for meeting certain types of medical expenses of the aged through OASDI, the net result would be an increase in total amounts expended through public and private channels on the medical care of elderly beneficiaries. The implications for housing expenditures are more clear-cut. It is apparent that one of the most significant effects of OASDI, along with other income-maintenance programs, has been to facilitate the maintenance of separate households by families and individuals who would otherwise be living with relatives or in rooming houses.[18] Further-

[18]During the period from 1947 to 1961, the number of married couples who were not living in their own households declined from about

more, the expansion of OASDI and other retirement income programs has facilitated the geographical mobility of older persons and is undoubtedly a factor in encouraging movement to Florida, California, and other areas with mild climates. Tendencies in these directions would probably be even more pronounced were it not for the gap between average OASDI benefits and budgetary requirements, to be discussed below.

In any analysis of the impact of the changing income status of the aged on the housing market, it is important, also, to take account of the long-run increase in home-ownership in younger age brackets. Future cohorts of elderly couples and individuals will be more likely to own homes than present cohorts (108). This will have significant implications, not only for the housing market, but for the budgetary requirements of the aged in the future.

COUNTERCYCLICAL EFFECTS

Although the countercyclical effects of unemployment insurance are widely appreciated, the countercyclical effects of OASDI have received less attention. During an upswing, *celeris paribus,* OASDI revenue will rise along with the expansion of payrolls, while expenditures will be held back (71) to the extent that potential beneficiaries sacrifice benefits to take advantage of more favorable employment opportunities (the employment effect). Furthermore, in a system in which there is no provision for automatic adjustment of benefit levels to changing price or wage levels [and even, to some extent, in one in which there is (69)] increases in benefit levels may lag behind increases in wages, which will hold down benefit payments in relation to contribu-

---

three million to about one million, or from nearly 8.7 percent of all married couples to 2.4 percent (215). The extent of the change in the household status of individuals cannot be directly determined from the data, nor are they available by age, but earlier data indicate that between 1947 and 1953 the proportion of men and women aged 65 and over who were classified as household heads or wives of heads rose, while the proportion classified as "other relatives of head" declined. These trends have also, of course, been influenced by the tendency for average real income to increase.

tions during an upswing (the wage effect).[19] The employment effect is likely to operate in the reverse manner in a recession, but the wage effect may not. It should be noted that these effects are not dependent on an excess of benefits over contributions developing in a depression. It is the *change* in the relationship between contributions and benefits that is significant.[20]

Economists who have sought to develop estimates of the countercyclical impact of OASDI have concluded that the strength of the upward trend in contributions and expenditures—reflecting the immaturity of the program and the effects of frequent statutory changes of a liberalizing character—has tended to swamp any possible countercyclical effects (7 and 13). However, these studies were based on data up to about 1957 and did not take account of developments during the 1957-58 recession, when, for the first time, expenditures for old-age and survivors benefits (but not for disability benefits) exceeded contributions.[21] As the program matures, it may be anticipated that its countercyclical effects will become more significant.

----

[19]Where the earnings base is below average full-time earnings, as in the case of OASDI, the wage effect may not operate.

[20]There is another complication, however, which must be taken into account in analyzing the countercyclical effects of changes in OASDI contributions and benefit payments. The fact that OASDI trust funds may have to increase their purchases of government bonds in an upswing and sell government bonds in a downswing will tend to affect the supply of loanable funds and interest rates and may conceivably have effects on investment that counteract, at least partly, the effects of changes in the relationship between contributions and benefit payments, since money-market effects may operate in a reverse direction—stimulating investment in an upswing and deterring it in a downswing. To some extent, these effects may be offset through appropriate monetary policies. The net effects are likely to depend on whether the impact on the marginal efficiency of capital is strong or weak as compared with the impact on liquidity preference (6, 64, and 65).

[21]Moreover, when contributions to the OASDI and DI trust funds are adjusted to reflect accurately the amounts that actually accrued in given years, rather than the manner in which they are originally recorded by the Treasury, it is found that total contributions declined between 1957 and 1958 and rose between 1958 and 1959 more sharply than the usual published figures indicate (135).

Occasionally, economists have suggested enhancing the countercyclical effects of social insurance programs through raising contributory tax rates in upswings and lowering them in downswings (76), whereas other writers (74) have stressed the advantages of stable contributory tax rates which would be set in such a way that contributions and benefits would have a neutral effect on consumption under conditions of full employment and a stimulating effect at less than full employment. These questions are interrelated with other financing issues which will be considered in a later section. Thus far, Congress has shown little disposition to consider a system of financing which would have stronger countercyclical effects, but it has shown some tendency to speed the adoption of liberalizing amendments at times when they would serve to spur recovery from depression, as in early 1961. Clearly, the stimulating effect on aggregate spending will, in such cases, be considerably more pronounced if increases in contributory taxes to finance the increased benefits are deferred to a later date. The possibilities inherent in this type of countercyclical fiscal policy have received far too little attention from economists, nor has there been enough discussion of the advantages and disadvantages of such action versus, say, a tax cut, in terms of the impact on persons in various income groups.

THE DETERMINATION OF BENEFIT LEVELS

If, as the previous discussion has suggested, OASDI has significant effects on labor force participation, productivity, consumption, and economic stability, it is also clear that the magnitude of these effects will depend in considerable measure on the relationship between average benefits and price and wage levels. Yet, except for a limited number of social security experts, few economists have concerned themselves with the question of OASDI benefit levels.

As J. Douglas Brown (54) has emphasized, an important element in the American philosophy of social insurance is that benefits should be related to previous earnings, thereby enhancing the incentive of workers to strive for high and continuous earnings. This is in sharp contrast to the British egalitarian tradition

of flat benefits, providing a minimum subsistence level, which
was endorsed in the writings of the Fabian Socialists and in the
Beveridge Report, but has come increasingly under question in
recent years (53, 82, and 121).

In practice, the principle of relating benefits to previous
earnings in OASDI has been extensively modified in favor of the
conflicting principle of providing a basic "floor of protection."
As a result, it is not a serious exaggeration to maintain that our
benefit structure bears greater resemblance to a flat-benefit system than to an earnings-related system of, say, the type found in
West Germany (42, p. 559).

It is not simply that the benefit formula is heavily weighted
in favor of the low earner. Numerous other features of OASDI
have the effect of modifying the principle of relating benefits to
earnings: the provisions for minimum and maximum benefits; the
fact that increases in the earnings base have applied only to
earnings after the effective date of the amendment (a logical feature in a contributory system); the limited number of quarters required for fully insured status (favoring the worker with a seasonal or intermittent work pattern); and the fact that only in the
most restricted sense, at present, does a worker who retires after
a long period of coverage have any advantage over one who has
had the same rate of earnings but minimal quarters of coverage.[22]

The fact that benefits are paid to dependents represents, of

[22]In principle, a worker with a steady earnings pattern and a long
period of coverage has an advantage because he will not have experienced periods of unemployment or periods out of the labor force which
would adversely affect his average monthly wage. In practice, the fact
that the computation can begin at the end of 1950 (which is to the advantage of most persons retiring today because of the upward wage trend)
and the fact that the five years of lowest earnings can be dropped out
means that the man who worked steadily from the end of 1950, to, say,
the end of 1961 may conceivably have no advantage over the individual
with only six years of earnings during this same period (assuming the
same rate of earnings and no disadvantage for the six-year man because
his earnings were concentrated in the early part of the period when the
ceiling on the average monthly wage was lower). As time goes on, this
will be less true, if no change is made in either the starting date or the
length of the drop-out period.

course, an additional modification based on the criterion of need, but this feature is found in nearly every country, whether or not the country has an earnings-related or a flat-benefit system.

Partly because of the substantial time lag between an increase in the earnings base and its full reflection in the computed average monthly wage of those applying for benefits, the proportion of beneficiaries receiving the maximum benefit has tended to be very small. By the end of 1960, the theoretical maximum benefit (corresponding to an average monthly wage of $400) had been $127 for two years, but the operating maximum was about $120, and less than 10 percent of those receiving retired worker's benefits were getting $116 a month or more. The average retired worker's benefit was $74.04, and nearly 60 percent were receiving from $45 to $105.

Although benefit increases have more than kept pace with increases in the consumer price index (124), on the average, since 1940 (lagging behind, however, during the decade of the forties), average benefits are slightly lower in relation to earnings levels than they were two decades ago.[23]

The undesirability of stationary benefit levels in a period of persistent price and wage increases has forced most countries to consider various methods of adjusting benefit levels upward in their social security programs in the postwar period. The problem is more complex in a contributory social insurance program providing long-term pension payments than in a program providing short-term benefits, since contributions are usually made over a working life during which earnings may rise markedly and benefits are paid over a considerable period of years.

Should benefits be adjusted to changes in consumer prices, thereby presumably stabilizing the level of living of the beneficiaries, or should they be adjusted to wage increases, thereby permitting beneficiaries to share in rising real income? This question has increasingly come to the forefront in debates over revision of old-age insurance systems in numerous countries in

[23]For example, the average retired worker's monthly benefit of $22.60 represented 20.8 percent of average monthly earnings in manufacturing in 1940, while the average benefit of $74.04 represented 18.9 percent of average factory earnings in 1960.

recent years, and thus far has been answered quite differently in various countries. Clearly, in view of the tendency for real income to increase over time, adjusting benefits to wage changes will appear to be more costly than adjusting them to consumer price changes. However, in practice, a decision to adjust benefits to consumer price levels cannot be assumed to "freeze" the level of living of the beneficiaries indefinitely, since much will depend on the accuracy with which the consumer price index measures cost-of-living changes and the manner in which beneficiaries are affected by revisions in the index.[24] Moreover, in the long run, there is likely to be strong pressure either toward adoption of a system designed to adjust benefits to current wage levels, as in West Germany and Sweden, or toward periodic increases in benefit levels to reflect increases in real income. From the point of view of economic analysis, it is important to recognize that these pressures will stem, not merely from whatever political influence the pensioners themselves may exert, but from the close social and economic ties between the pensioners and the rest of society. If the value of pension benefits is suffering serious erosion in relation to real earnings levels, employed middle-aged adults will in many cases feel increasing compunction to assist aged parents or other relatives who cannot afford consumption items they regard as essential, e.g., adequate medical care. Thus, in their own immediate self-interest, quite apart from broader social objectives or regard for their prospective retirement income, they are likely to be impelled toward support of more adequate pensions.

Thus far, Congress has shied away from any proposal to adjust OASDI benefits automatically to either price or wage changes, but it *has* shown a tendency, particularly in relatively recent years, to adjust benefits upward proportionately with increases in the consumer price index, though with some lag. In view of the fact that the aged—by far the most numerous class of beneficiaries—have quite different consumption patterns from younger families, the question has sometimes been raised whether a spe-

[24]For discussions of the tendency for budgetary standards to be revised upward as real income increases, see 1 and 30.

cial cost-of-living index for the aged should be constructed and used as a criterion for benefit changes. Given the relatively pronounced increases in certain items that figure comparatively prominently in the budgets of elderly people, particularly the costs of medical care, during the last decade, such a procedure might have made a marked difference. When the U. S. Bureau of Labor Statistics recently published its interim revision of the special budget for elderly couples living in rented quarters in 20 large cities (93, 123, and 130), it also published estimates of the 1959 cost of the original elderly couple's budget, which had first been published in 1948 and last repriced in October, 1950. The cost of the original budget in the autumn of 1959 ranged from $2,390 in Houston to $3,110 in Chicago, reflecting increases, as compared with the autumn of 1950, ranging from 29 percent in Houston to 71 percent in Chicago and averaging 59 percent for the 20 cities. During the same period, the BLS consumer price index rose 20 percent.

Although costs have probably risen less for elderly homeowners than for renters, since the rent component of the consumer price index has increased more than the total housing component, it should be recognized that the proportion of homeowners in the elderly population is not as high in large cities as it is in smaller communities. Nevertheless, merely raising this question points to one of the difficulties involved in any consideration of a specialized consumer price index. The impact of price changes on the elderly during the last decade has probably varied considerably, not only for home-owners and renters, but also for those living in large cities and in smaller communities. We need much more information on all these variations before considering the use of a specialized index (49). It is worth noting, moreover, that the need for specialized budgets and indexes is even more acute in connection with the administration of the public assistance program than it is in OASDI.

The proposal to include provision for the financing of selected medical expenses of elderly people in the OASDI program originated, of course, largely as a result of the relatively rapid increase in the cost of medical care during the fifties, along with recognition of the fact that elderly people are particularly likely to incur medical expenses, especially for prolonged illnesses (99). It is anticipated that costs of medical care will continue to increase somewhat more rapidly than most other components of the consumer price index in the future. Thus, if Congress should adopt legislation of the Anderson-King type, the effect would be to shift at least part of the burden of rising medical costs from the aged to employed persons.

The revised elderly couple's budget suggests that, at least in some large cities, average OASDI benefits received by elderly couples represent less than half of the annual amount needed by an elderly couple living in rented quarters for a "modest, but adequate" level of living. In San Francisco, for example, average OASDI benefits received by elderly couples at the end of 1960 were about $130 a month, or $1,560 a year, while the revised budget (as of the autumn of 1959) was $3,223.[25] If we assume that housing costs for elderly home-owners without a mortgage average 30 percent lower than for renters (96, p. 90n), as data from the 1957 old-age beneficiary survey suggest, the budgetary figure for elderly couples owning their own homes free and clear in San Francisco would have been $2,871 in late 1959.

However, it should also be recognized that some beneficiaries, who are eligible for benefits under several programs, may do exceedingly well. There is a growing problem of overlapping and duplication of benefits which we have not as yet squarely faced. Some European countries, e.g., Norway, have worked out very careful provisions under which persons entitled to benefits under two programs will get all of one benefit and part of another, but not all of both.

[25]Average benefits for retired workers in San Francisco in December, 1960 were $78.82, while the average OASDI wife's or husband's benefit was $43.29. Since retired workers include a good many persons without a spouse whose benefits, particularly in the case of women, tend to be lower than those of married men, multiplying the average wife's or husband's benefit, which is always 50 percent of the primary benefit, by three would appear to provide the best basis for estimating the elderly couple's average benefit. (The data were supplied by the San Francisco Regional Office of the Social Security Administration.)

How far should OASDI benefits go toward providing an adequate level of living for beneficiaries, and to what extent should their needs be met from other sources, such as personal savings and private pension plans? Or, in other words, what, precisely, do we mean by a "basic floor of protection"? On this question of central importance, opinions differ widely. Although congressional decisions will always depend, ultimately, on political forces, the economist can play a role in clarifying the issues involved.

Few would argue that the average wage-earner can be expected to accumulate, through individual saving during his working life, a large enough sum to provide a substantial supplement to his social security benefits in retirement. Although this might be feasible at some time in the future, only a small proportion of couples or individuals approaching retirement age today have financial assets in the amounts that would be required to provide an appreciable supplement to OASDI benefit payments.[26]

However, our public policy, particularly since World War II, has provided strong support for the expansion and liberalization of private pension plans, which do play an important role in supplementing OASDI benefits for a minority of retirees. Employer contributions to private pension plans are tax exempt, provided the plans meet certain standards imposed by the Bureau of Internal Revenue, although we do not go as far as the British in providing tax exemption for employee contributions as well.[27]

There is little question, also, that at least part of the impetus for expansion of private pensions has been associated with recognition of the fact that social security benefits are too low to provide for budgetary needs in retirement. This has been particularly clear in connection with the union drive for collectively bargained plans.

[26]See, for example, the data on liquid assets in 51.

[27]In addition, since the Supreme Court's decision in the Inland Steel case, pension plans have been recognized as a legitimate subject for collective bargaining under the National Labor-Management Relations Act. Furthermore, wage stabilization policies during World War II and the Korean War encouraged employer contributions to "fringe benefit" plans as a substitute for direct wage increases.

Many questions have been raised about the relative roles of OASDI and private pension plans in recent years, and there has been an encouraging increase in research on the economic implications of private pension plans.

Any attempt to discuss the findings of this research would take us too far afield, but some of the questions that are being asked about private pension plans are highly relevant to a discussion of the relationship between OASDI benefit levels and private pensions. What are the chances, for example, that those who are not now covered by private pension plans—totaling roughly two-thirds of the labor force and including particularly such groups as employees of small firms, the self-employed, farm workers, and domestic workers—will be covered in the future?[28] Is our reliance on private pensions to supplement minimal OASDI benefits leading to a situation, as Titmuss (87, Chap. 3) has argued with reference to Great Britain, in which income disparities in old age will be wider than in working life? What is the impact of private pensions on labor mobility? Should we consider legislation which would require the transferability of pension rights, and perhaps also provide for supplementary benefits comparable to private pension benefits for those not covered by private plans, in line with the 1959 amendments (122) to the British old-age insurance system? Should employee contributions to private plans be made tax exempt? What is the impact of pension fund accumulation on the economy?

Another extremely important set of questions, which has received relatively little attention, concerns the extent to which, given the low level of OASDI benefits in relation to the budgetary needs of beneficiaries, we are paying in other ways for needs which might conceivably be met at no greater cost by raising OASDI benefit levels.

The tax exemption of employer contributions to pension plans has already been mentioned. There are a number of provisions of the federal income tax law providing special tax privi-

28In 1962 Congress enacted legislation providing for tax exemption of contributions of the self-employed to a pension plan, with certain restrictions.

leges for persons aged 65 and over—larger personal exemptions, a special tax credit, and generous provisions for the deduction of medical expenses. Increasingly, state governments are enacting similar provisions and local governments are under pressure to provide special tax privileges for elderly home-owners. Early in 1960, about 7 percent of all aged OASDI beneficiaries were receiving supplementary old-age assistance payments because their benefits were insufficient to provide the level of living permitted under state old-age assistance provisions (which vary greatly from state to state), while about 4 percent of OASDI beneficiary families with children were receiving additional payments under the program for aid to dependent children (117). The new program of Medical Assistance to the Aged, adopted under the Kerr-Mills Act of 1960, is providing funds, in those states which have adopted implementing legislation, to meet at least part of the costs of medical care for the aged—many of them OASDI beneficiaries—who do not need cash old-age assistance payments but whose incomes are insufficient (under eligibility conditions determined by the states) to meet their medical costs. A sizable, and growing, number can qualify for veterans' benefits on the basis of an income test (115, 136). At least part of the pressure to provide various types of subsidies for housing for the elderly under federal legislation, and increasingly under laws enacted in the various states, is related to the incapacity of elderly persons to meet their housing costs (127). There is also increasing pressure for other special measures—not always involving public funds—such as reduced bus fares, reduced movie fares, and the like.

Each of the special tax exemptions and many of the special programs have been supported on the ground that elderly people are having great difficulty making ends meet. How strong would the residual case for them be if the income status of the aged were more satisfactory? What are the total costs involved, in relation to the cost of varying increases in OASDI benefit levels? What would be the implications for OASDI financing if a larger part of the burden were carried through OASDI? What savings might be effected in other public welfare expenditures if medical expenses of the aged were provided through OASDI? To what extent is it preferable to aim at increasing the real income of the aged through the provision of public services, as some of these programs do, and to what extent is it preferable to rely strictly on cash income-maintenance payments, on the ground that the recipient is thereby granted the maximum freedom of consumer choice (35 and 56, Introduction)? What are the implications with respect to the achievement of both adequacy and equity in welfare policies? Economists are particularly well equipped to tackle some of these questions, which have thus far received little attention.

In connection with all these issues, the question of how much of an expansion of OASDI the economy could afford and how it might be financed are obviously involved. Let us turn, therefore, to the financing issues.

FINANCING ISSUES

The most important issues associated with the financing of OASDI may be expressed in the form of three questions: What proportion of our resources can we afford to allocate to the program? How shall the costs, i.e., the tax burden, be distributed among various segments of the population? To what extent should funds be accumulated to meet the costs of the program in future years? [29] Since the first question is the most general one, it will be helpful to consider it first.

The allocation of resources to OASDI. Economists are often asked about the capacity of the economy to support increases in social security expenditures. There is no simple formula which will provide the answer to this question. Furthermore, as Mrs. Burns has pointed out, "the answer given by each country at any given time is a function of its economic situation, its social values and the nature and extent of competing demands on incomes that are secured through the operation of the economic market" (55, p. 9).

Nevertheless, the economist can make a major contribution

---

[29] For a somewhat similar list of questions, see 55.

to public debate on this issue by 1) warning against "rule of thumb" solutions, 2) showing how the tools of economic analysis can be used to clarify the issues, and 3) conducting empirical research designed to provide the facts that are relevant to intelligent decisions.

The desirability of *timing* changes in the program so as to maximize its contribution to economic stability has already been suggested. But the central issue is whether we can afford to add new types of benefits or make a substantial improvement in the benefit formula.[30]

There is little likelihood, judging from the experience of the recent past, that the present program will be cut back, even though, as it matures, its costs are likely to rise somewhat in relation to the national income. However, they will not rise as rapidly as was once expected, since the sustained high birth rates of the last two decades have led to very substantial revision of earlier forecasts indicating that the proportion of elderly people in the population would rise considerably above its present level (129, Chap. 2; and 188). It is also important to recognize that failure to raise the earnings base commensurately with increases in earnings levels involves erosion of benefits in relation to average earnings (in this sense, it is not clear that the present program will be maintained), and at the same time requires higher contributory tax rates than would be necessary if the earnings base were raised more rapidly. In the spring of 1961, the Chief Actuary indicated that if the earnings base were to bear the same relationship to earnings levels as did the original $3,000 base in the late 1930s, it would have to be somewhat over $10,000, rather than $4,800. Raising the base to that extent, he estimated, would permit financing the program then in effect with a reduction of one percentage point in the combined employer-employee tax rate, since, in view of the slanting of the

[30]The question of expanding coverage is no longer much of an issue, although there is still disagreement over such questions as whether persons in the present aged population who retired before they had a chance to achieve eligibility should be "blanketed in."

benefit formula in favor of low earners, contributions would rise
more than benefits.[31]

Many writers on social security issues take the position
that as real income rises an economy can afford to allocate a larger share of its resources to welfare programs. However, to the
extent that rising real income is associated with a decline in the
relative importance of poverty, the need for increasing the share
of social security may diminish after real income rises to a certain level (80, Chap. 3). While these general considerations are
of interest, particularly in connection with international comparisons, they do not help much in relation to policy decisions in a
particular country at a particular time.

Although transfer payments are not classified as public expenditures in the gross national product accounts, they do compete with other public programs for their share of the taxpayer's
dollar, and we shall include them when we refer to the public
sector. Substantially expanding OASDI expenditures would depend on allocating a larger share of total public expenditures to
the program or on allocating a larger share of our resources to
the public sector.

In view of the pressing needs for expenditures for defense,
foreign aid, education, and other programs to which most Ameri-
cans attach great importance, the prospects for substantially increasing the share of tax revenues allocated to OASDI do not appear promising in the near future unless the international situation improves. Our previous discussion has suggested, however,
that an informed public opinion will consider not only the needs
of OASDI beneficiaries but the potential contribution of the program to economic stability and economic growth. Furthermore, as
already suggested, economists could make a major contribution
to informed decision-making by analyzing the financial relationships among the various types of welfare programs and estimating
the savings that might be effected in other types of expenditures

[31]See 92, p. 51, for estimates of savings associated with increases
in the earnings base to various amounts up to $9,000. The estimate of a
saving of one percentage point associated with an increase in the earnings base to $10,000 was given to me by the Chief Actuary in an oral
conversation.

if OASDI benefits were increased by varying amounts. Indeed, there is an increasing need for a "social accounting" approach to the analysis of the complex interrelationships among welfare expenditures.

At present, it would be particularly useful to have estimates of the saving in welfare expenditures of all types (unemployment insurance, OASDI, public assistance, training and redevelopment programs, private welfare expenditures, etc.) which might be effected through a substantial reduction in the unemployment rate, as well as of the increases in tax revenues that would be associated with such a reduction. Much of the current hue and cry about high welfare expenditures tends to ignore the fact that unemployment is in part responsible for the increase that has occurred in the last few years.

What about the share of our resources that should be allocated to the public sector (including OASDI)? Principles such as maintaining a relatively constant total dollar volume of public expenditures (averaged over the business cycle) or allocating a constant percentage of the national income to the public sector clearly belong in the "rule-of-thumb" class. Samuelson (45-47) argues that the interrelations between public spending and private consumption and investment should always be kept in mind, and that the appropriate distribution of resources between the public and private sectors will depend on such factors as consumer preferences for public versus private goods and services, income distribution, and institutional arrangements. He criticizes particularly the view that the income elasticity of public services must be zero (a view which implies that expenditures on public services should be held at a constant dollar amount).

Such economists as Hansen and Galbraith treat this issue in less theoretical and more emphatic terms. Hansen (23 and 24) argues that since the proportion of income spent on services is rising rapidly at present levels of real income, and many types of services are best provided through the public sector, the proportion of the national income allocated to public services (including social security) should be substantially expanded in the 1960s. He also suggests that we have thought too much in terms of stimulating investment in material resources, with resulting neglect of the investment in human resources which can be accomplished through education and other public services. Galbraith's *The Affluent Society* (18) is widely known as an eloquent statement of the argument that the public sector is being starved in favor of bigger tailfins and a barbecue in every backyard. Striner (131) has recently argued that the economy could easily absorb a very marked increase in OASDI benefit levels.

The economists who resist this point of view, particularly those associated with the Montpelerin group,[32] fear the encroachment of big government in general, and "the welfare state" in particular, on the domain of private enterprise and individual liberty.

These differences, which are to a considerable extent ideological, are not likely to be fully resolved. But, as already suggested, economists can make an important contribution to analysis of the issues, particularly through carefully designed comparative studies of the impact of welfare expenditures on the economy in various countries.

The distribution of the tax burden. Should the tax burden be distributed, wholly or primarily, in accordance with the benefits that will be received from the program or in accordance with the principle of ability to pay? Each of these principles has a long and venerable history (40, Chaps. 4 and 5) in the development of the theory of public finance, and both, in varying degrees and combinations, have influenced methods of financing social security systems in various countries.

It is clear that the first of these principles is predominant in the financing of OASDI. The compulsory contributory taxes are paid by the prospective beneficiaries and their employers. To be sure, the payments are proportional to earnings, but only up to the earnings ceiling. However, the distribution of benefits among beneficiaries is, as we have seen, by no means proportional to the contributions which they or their employers have made. If

[32]Prominent in this group, which takes its name from a meeting held at Montpelerin, Switzerland, are such economists as Friedman, Hayek, Machlup, and von Mises.

both contributions and benefits are taken into account, the system has a substantial redistributional effect.

The general principle that OASDI should be financed primarily by contributory taxes is seldom questioned, but there is a substantial body of opinion, perhaps particularly among economists, in favor of providing part of the support for the program through general government revenues, rather than relying solely on contributory taxes. The issues can best be clarified by considering the arguments pro and con a substantial contribution from general government revenues.

In favor of some degree of support for the program from general government revenues, the following arguments have been advanced.

1. The contributory taxes are regressive in their impact, particularly when account is taken of the shifting of the employer portion of the tax. The extent to which the employer will be in a position to pass the tax along to the consumer in the form of a higher price will vary with business conditions, the character of the demand for the product (whether it is elastic or inelastic), and other factors,[33] but the strength of inflationary forces in the last few decades has been such that most employers have probably been in a position most of the time to respond to an increase in the payroll tax by raising the prices on their products. Under these conditions employees also pay the employer portion of the tax in their capacity as consumers, though its incidence will be somewhat different from that of the employee contribution. Greater reliance on general revenues of the federal government, derived primarily from the progressive income tax and the corporate profits tax, would result in distributing the OASDI tax burden more in accordance with ability to pay and would thus enhance the income-redistribution effects of the program.

2. When the employer encounters consumer resistance to price increases, because of a recession, foreign competition, or

[33]For an extensive discussion of the impact of payroll taxes, see 65, Part II. The recent literature on tax shifting and tax incidence has emphasized the importance of treating the problem in general equilibrium rather than partial equilibrium terms (40, Part 3; and 43).

for other reasons, he is likely to attempt to shift the payroll tax to his employees by resisting wage increases or by introducing labor-saving changes in production methods which will make possible a reduction in his work force. This type of response has probably been more prevalent in the late 1950s and early 1960s than previously because of increased concern over foreign competition and consumer resistance to higher prices. The problem would be less serious if OASDI were the only program imposing a payroll tax, but unemployment insurance is financed exclusively by a payroll tax in most states, while workmen's compensation is financed by premium payments based on the employer's payroll and the degree of accident risk in the industry. Furthermore, employers have been under increasing pressure to expand private "fringe benefits." Thus, OASDI contributory taxes tend to be viewed by employers as simply one element in a wide assortment of fringe payments, which, according to a U. S. Chamber of Commerce study, increased from 3 percent of payrolls, on the average, in 1929 to 19 percent in 1959, and in the latter year ran up as high as 50 percent or more for some firms (165).[34] The problem is not so much one in which increases in OASDI tax rates will by themselves have a substantially adverse effect on employment as one in which constant upward pressure on fringes of all types as well as on direct wage payments is leading employers to turn more and more to labor-saving changes in production methods.

3. The contributory OASDI taxes have the disadvantage, in common with other types of earmarked sources of revenue, of limiting the power of Congress to determine how much should be spent on OASDI in relation to all other government programs. The amount available from the earmarked source at any particular time may be more or less than Congress might have appropriated for the program if the amounts had had to come at least partly out

---

[34]These percentages are based on estimates of total fringe payments in public and private employment as a proportion of total wages and salaries. For firms actually included in the Chamber of Commerce Survey, fringe payments averaged 22.8 percent of payroll in 1959 and had increased to 24.9 percent in 1961 (165 and 166).

of general government revenues. In other words, Congress would be more likely to vary expenditures on the program in the light of needs of the beneficiaries and the impact of the program on the economy if a portion of the funds were appropriated from general revenues as is done in many European countries (76, pp. 101-2).

4. It is inconsistent with the general purpose of contributory taxes to force workers who will be covered by the program over a long period of years to pay taxes which reflect the full costs of unearned benefits of persons who have retired or will retire on the basis of minimal periods of coverage. As Mrs. Burns has pointed out, these unearned benefits represent a level premium cost amounting to 3½ percent of payroll, which might more logically have been financed out of general government revenues, since they are a responsibility of society as a whole rather than of the present generation of younger workers (55, p. 13-14).

Those who strongly support contributory taxes and would either oppose any contribution from general revenues or restrict such a contribution to a very minor role make the following points.[35]

1. Financing the program wholly or almost entirely through contributory taxes has important psychological advantages. People feel they have earned their benefits (even when a substantial portion is unearned), that they are receiving them as a matter of right, and that their benefits are not a government "handout."

2. If OASDI benefits were financed to any appreciable extent from general government revenues, it would be difficult to provide anything more than a bare subsistence level of benefits, since those with relatively high incomes would object to providing any more than this through a welfare program to which they would be contributing far more than they were getting back.

3. In a period of rising price and wage levels, benefits can be increased under a contributory system without raising tax rates. If benefits are financed to a considerable extent through general revenues, it may be more difficult to obtain increases,

[35]For a well-known statement of the arguments for contributory taxes, see 82, p. 108.

since, though tax revenues will increase, the social security program will have to compete with all other government programs for
its share of expanding appropriations.[36]

4. It is easier to obtain an increase in contributory taxes
than in a progressive income tax, since less voter resistance
seems to be offered, and any proposal to increase income taxes
leads to a legislative morass growing out of controversy as to
how the increase should be distributed among income groups.[37]

To sum up the situation, the generally favorable experience
with earnings-related contributory taxes in the last few decades
has played a significant role in inducing a shift of sentiment,
both on the part of economists and other groups, away from former
antipathy based on their regressive character. Nevertheless, the
likelihood that a combination of payroll taxes plus employer contributions to private employee benefit plans is having adverse
effects on employment, at least in the short run, is a problem of
growing concern, and there are strong arguments for some type of
contribution to OASDI from general government revenues, as is
the common practice in the financing of social insurance schemes
in western Europe.

The problem of fund accumulation. A private insurance program must be financed in such a way as to be self-sustaining.
The implications of this principle for private old-age insurance

[36]Between 1950 and 1957, there was a tendency for benefit levels
in old-age pension programs to increase more, in relation to per capita
income, in countries relying primarily on contributory, earnings-related
taxes than in countries where the program was financed through general
revenues or a combination of general revenues and flat contributions,
as in Britain. See 109.

[37]This argument is adapted from the arguments in favor of a sales
tax presented by Galbraith (18). He also argued that in view of the fact
that we were allocating too large a proportion of our resources to the
production of consumer goods a sales tax would have the virtue of restricting consumption. Similar arguments apply to the payroll tax in a
period when the employer can readily pass the tax on to the consumer,
but, in a period in which the employer may be more likely to respond to
an increase in a payroll tax by restricting employment, the sales taxes
and payroll taxes may have somewhat dissimilar effects.

programs have been expressed as follows by a leading actuary (112, p. 41):

In private old-age insurance, reserves must be built up from premiums collected in order to provide the funds necessary to permit the ultimate payment of all annuities as they individually and collectively fall due over the years, whether membership in the insured group or groups increases, decreases, or ceases.

Full-reserve financing in the private insurance sense is not necessary for a social insurance program (97 and 112), since 1) it is operated on the assumption that it will be continued on a permanent basis, 2) coverage is compulsory, and the government need not allow for the possibility, as a private insurance company must, that insured persons will shift their patronage to other insurers, and 3) if accumulated funds turn out to be inadequate to meet liabilities at any time, the government may raise contributory taxes or meet the deficit in the program through an appropriation from general revenues.

The financing provisions of OASDI have represented a compromise between full-reserve financing and pay-as-you-go financing (70). The prospect that costs would rise as the program matured has been met through a schedule of contributory taxes that called for gradual increases, but the rates in effect over most of the period since the program was initiated have been somewhat higher than those that would have been required on a pay-as-you-go basis. The result has been the accumulation of a fund which, together with accrued interest, is currently roughly twice as large as annual OASDI expenditures and will, on the basis of the present financing plan, rise to substantially higher levels in the future (see Table 8).

The economic implications of fund accumulation have been extensively analyzed by economists (65, 94, and 97). A good many have expressed doubts about the wisdom of the accumulation of a sizable trust fund on various grounds, of which perhaps the most important have been: 1) trust-fund accumulation is likely to have a deflationary impact on the economy unless the demand for investment funds is strong enough to offset the effects of the

withdrawal of funds from consumers,[38] and 2) the effort to reduce
the financial burden for future generations through fund accumulation will prove illusory if the deflationary impact slows down
the rate of growth of the real gross national product. Counter-
arguments have been advanced to the effect that the investment
of the reserves is likely *in fact* to stimulate capital formation,
which will increase the rate of growth of real GNP and thus increase the capacity of the economy to support OASDI in the future (45, 76, and 94). Nearly all economists writing on this subject have recognized that there are noneconomic arguments for
some degree of fund accumulation which need to be given some
weight. In practice, as we have seen, to the extent that OASDI
fund accumulation may have had a deflationary impact on the
economy from the late 1930s to about 1955, the effects were desirable in a period characterized by strong inflationary tendencies.

In recent years, OASDI revenues and expenditures have been
in fairly close balance and, as suggested earlier, the net effects
may have been somewhat inflationary. But, as Carroll (94) warns,
the current financing plan calls for a substantial excess of
revenues over expenditures in the latter part of the present decade. Whether such a development will be in the interests of the
economy will depend largely on whether the current problem of
persistent unemployment has, by then, been overcome and inflationary tendencies have again become predominant. If not, there
will be an opportunity for Congress to reconsider the tax increases currently scheduled for 1966 and 1968. Given the large
element of uncertainty as to whether trust-fund accumulation can
actually accomplish its purposes, the case for making decisions
about changes in benefit and financing provisions in the light of
the economic conditions prevailing at any given time would appear to be quite strong, particularly since the program has now
developed to a point at which the differences in total contribu-

---

[38]Furthermore, as already suggested in discussing countercyclical
effects, the money-market effects of investing the reserve might be ex-
pansionary.

tions implied by present OASDI principles as compared with pay-as-you-go principles are not very great.[39]

Finally, it is apparent that the three financing issues which we have considered are interrelated. Whether or not reserve financing is followed, and to what extent, clearly has implications for the capacity of the economy to afford the program at any given time and for the distribution of the tax burden.

SUMMARY

A great deal of work remains to be done before economists will have developed an adequate interpretation of the impact of a long-term insurance program like OASDI on the economy, either in this country or abroad. Although financing issues have been extensively discussed in the literature, other issues have been almost entirely neglected, except by a few social security experts. Yet there are indications that the program may have a significant effect on economic growth, partly through its impact on human resources and on the adjustment of the labor force to economic change, and that these effects might be enhanced through appropriately framed amendments. Moreover, there is evidence that with contributions and expenditures approximately in balance the transfers effected through OASDI stimulate an increase in aggregate consumption expenditures, and that timing liberalizing amendments so that they take effect during recessions can be a useful countercyclical device. Furthermore, as the program matures, its role as an automatic stabilizer is likely to become more significant.

Whether OASDI has had any longer-run effects on consumer behavior is less clear. Progress toward more adequate analysis of this question will depend partly on further development of the theory of the consumption function and partly on more intensive empirical research. A promising method of inquiry that has been almost totally neglected is comparative analysis of the impact of

[39]One of the elements of uncertainty which we have not discussed has to do with the problems involved in estimating future costs of the program. For discussion of these problems, see 94, 103, and 114.

various types of welfare programs, including old-age insurance programs, on the economy in various countries. Even more neglected has been any attempt to analyze the interaction between OASDI and other public welfare expenditures. Yet legislative decisions are constantly being made on the basis of estimates that consider only the direct costs or savings associated with a particular change, without any reference to indirect costs or savings that might be associated with it.

5. UNEMPLOYMENT COMPENSATION

Although far-reaching changes in OASDI are unlikely, the situation may be somewhat different in unemployment compensation. Both the Area Redevelopment Act of 1961 and the Manpower Development and Training Act of 1962 provide federal funds for retraining programs for jobless workers, while the Trade Expansion Act of 1962 provides adjustment benefits for workers displaced as a result of tariff reductions. Other proposals which have been before Congress in the last few years—legislation to reform the federal-state unemployment system and to improve employment opportunities for young people—would also, if enacted, have highly significant effects on the compensation of the unemployed.

Given the concern over an uncomfortably high unemployment rate in recent years, it is scarcely surprising that proposals to provide more adequately for the unemployed have burgeoned. In fact, we have been hearing more and more discussion of the need to integrate the existing program, which is designed primarily to tide the jobless worker over a relatively short period of unemployment, with a broader set of labor market policies which would be built around the objective of restoring the unemployed worker to employment.[1]

[1]In workmen's compensation, we are somewhat further along the road to a similar shift in attitude. Originally designed as a scheme for indemnifying the injured worker, workmen's compensation is coming to be viewed increasingly as a program which should be built around the concept of restoring the injured worker to employment, although this shift in attitude took place much earlier in some European countries than in this country (58).

A number of European countries have moved a good deal further than we have in this direction. Sweden is perhaps best known for its particularly broad and successful labor market policies. Could comparable success be achieved in this country through changes modeled after the Swedish approach? Clearly the obstacles are numerous—the far greater size of the country, the complexity of federal-state relationships, the recent retardation of our rate of economic growth, and other factors. But before considering further the issue of changes in labor market policies in general, or how the unemployment insurance system would have to be altered to fit into such a program, we need to consider the economic effects of the present system, with all its strengths and weaknesses.

In his recently published study of the economics of unemployment compensation, Professor Lester (177, p. 4) has summarized the chief purposes of the American federal-state system as follows:

> Among the main aims of unemployment compensation are: (1) to provide a measure of economic security for wage-earners and their families through adequate partial compensation for wage loss from involuntary unemployment, (2) to cushion economic slumps and prevent spiralling unemployment by helping to maintain workers' purchasing power, and (3) to stimulate regularity of employment on the part of individual firms by means of incentive tax provisions. Less prominent purposes include: (1) fair and equitable distribution of the costs of unemployment, (2) preservation of work skills, (3) assurance of compensation as a matter of right to those regularly attached to the labor market, and (4) maintenance of normal economic incentives.

Although this is quite satisfactory as a summary of the purposes of the existing American system, in a somewhat broader context it would require some minor modifications. In view of the growing emphasis on the desirability of investment in human resources as a means of encouraging economic growth, for example, one might suggest that "preservation of work skills, *ought* to be one of the main aims of the system, even though it may not have been given major emphasis thus far. Furthermore, "stimulating regularity of employment on the part of individual firms by means of incentive tax provisions" is regarded as an important purpose of unemployment insurance in the United States, but comparable incentive tax provisions are not found in the unemployment insurance systems of other countries.

Nevertheless, we shall be guided by Lester's summary to some extent in organizing our discussion of the effects of the system.

INCOME AND CONSUMPTION EFFECTS

What proportion of the wage loss associated with unemployment is restored through the federal-state unemployment insurance system? The impact of the program on income and consumption will depend to a considerable extent on the answer to this question. Clearly, since four out of ten persons in the labor force, and about one out of five employees in private industry, are not covered by unemployment insurance, and since some covered workers who experience involuntary unemployment do not receive benefits for one reason or another, the proportion of wage loss restored to all the unemployed is bound to be a good deal lower than the proportion restored to those who actually receive benefits.

Experience of beneficiaries. Let us consider, first, the extent to which *beneficiaries* are compensated for their wage loss. Although most state laws aim at providing weekly benefits to totally unemployed workers that are equal to approximately half of a worker's previous full-time weekly earnings, the average weekly benefit actually received by a beneficiary during a period of unemployment tends to be considerably less than 50 percent of lost earnings in a large proportion of cases for a number of reasons:

1. All the states have provisions setting a maximum on the benefit amount, and, although these maxima have been increased from time to time, as wage levels have risen, there has been a tendency for the increases in maxima to lag behind wage increases (see Appendix).

2. On the average, the number of weeks for which unemployed workers are compensated tends to be somewhat lower than the actual number of weeks of unemployment experienced, because of the impact of waiting periods, delays in applying for benefits, periods of disqualification, and limitations on duration of benefits.

3. In some cases, jobless workers may not have worked full-time throughout the period which is used as a base in computing their average weekly wage, or their wages may have risen since that period and thus their benefits may be based on an average wage that is below their normal full-time weekly earnings.

Largely as a result of the erosion of maxima, average weekly benefits declined from 42 percent of average weekly earnings in 1939 to 35 percent in 1959 (205, p. 12).[2] These data, which relate average benefits paid during weeks of compensation to average earnings of covered workers, do not tell us what proportion of lost wages was actually restored to beneficiaries (whose wages tend to be somewhat lower than those of all covered workers) or how this proportion varied among various types of beneficiaries. For information on these questions, we must turn to the various beneficiary surveys that have been conducted in recent years, of which the most important are a group of surveys conducted by six state agencies in cooperation with the U.S. Bureau of Employment Security in selected labor market areas from 1954 to 1958 (204).

Each of the surveys, which were conducted along similar lines, was based on a sample of about 300 claimants who had been unemployed at least 6 weeks or more but were still receiving benefits (their average duration of unemployment, in the surveys which included this information, was about 17 weeks). Thus, those unemployed for very short periods, as well as exhaustees, were excluded. The samples were also restricted to single bene-

---

[2] Actually, the ratio of average weekly benefits to average weekly earnings reached a low point in the middle 1950s and increased slightly thereafter.

ficiaries and beneficiaries who were members of four-person families.[3]

The results of the studies were, on the whole, remarkably similar, although there were differences in the benefits received in the various areas, largely reflecting differences in benefit provisions of state laws, as well as a few other variations that will be noted below. The studies showed the following results.

1. Weekly benefit rates for most beneficiaries were less than half their former gross weekly earnings and in many cases were less than half their take-home pay.

2. The ratio of benefits to wages tended to be particularly low for primary wage-earners (heads of families), while single beneficiaries fared somewhat better, and there was a tendency for ratios of benefits to wages to be highest for secondary wage-earners. The relatively low benefit ratio for primary earners reflected their higher earnings and the fact that their benefits were more likely to be held down by restrictive maxima.[4]

3. Although most beneficiary family units received some income from sources other than unemployment benefits during unemployment, the amounts received were usually very modest, unless there was a second earner in the family. Average cash monthly income during unemployment for families of primary wage-earners and for single beneficiaries was less than half of cash income before unemployment in nearly all the surveys. The families of secondary wage-earners fared much better, since the chief breadwinner was generally at work.[5]

4. Reductions in family expenditures during unemployment were considerably less pronounced than income losses. Thus,

[3]The Albany-Schenectady-Troy study included a small number of three-person families.

[4]In the Portland, Oregon survey, for example, 76 percent of the primary earners qualified for the maximum benefit amount of $40, and 53 percent of these claimants received a weekly benefit amount that was less than 40 percent of their average gross weekly earnings.

[5]In the New York study, it was found that among single claimants and families with the sole wage-earner unemployed nearly three out of ten had no source of income other than unemployment benefits during unemployment.

the consumption behavior of these families was consistent with both the Duesenberry (12) hypothesis that consumption tends to be related to previous peak income and with the Friedman (17) hypothesis that consumption is a function of permanent income. Substantial proportions of the families maintained expenditures considerably above income by decreasing or exhausting savings, borrowing money, letting bills pile up (particularly indebtedness to stores), and receiving help from relatives or friends. Cash relief or relief in kind was received in relatively few cases.

5. Reductions in family expenditures tended to be larger for the beneficiaries surveyed during recessions than for those surveyed during more prosperous periods.[6] This appeared to reflect the less optimistic attitudes of beneficiaries surveyed during recessions toward prospects of reemployment of the unemployed family member, rather than more pronounced cuts in income or longer unemployment actually experienced up to the time of the survey (144, p. 39; and 177, p. 35).

6. For the families of primary earners, the average weekly benefit amount was considerably less than half of average weekly cash outlays in all the surveys—ranging from 38 percent in Tampa-St. Petersburg (1956) to 48 percent in Pittsburgh (1954). Benefit amounts went considerably further toward meeting nondeferrable expenditures—defined in these surveys as including food, shelter, utilities, and medical care—representing proportions ranging from more than half to more than three-quarters of nondeferrable expenses, depending on the survey.[7]

7. Patterns of expenditure reductions varied, but in the three recession surveys the most substantial reductions in terms

[6]In Albany-Schenectady-Troy, for example, where the survey was conducted in the spring of 1957, families of primary earners cut their cash outlays only 10 percent during unemployment, on the average, whereas in Portland, Oregon, where the survey was conducted in the spring of 1958, the average reduction in cash outlay for the families of primary earners amounted to 22 percent.

[7]For the single beneficiaries, benefit amounts compared much more favorably with cash outlays, while for the families of the secondary wage-earners they played a much less critical role.

of dollar amounts, for families of primary earners, tended to be made in outlays for food, housing and utilities, and transportation.

How do families of the unemployed fare when benefit rights are exhausted? The Haber-Cohen-Mueller study of unemployment in the 1958 recession provided some interesting information on how family adjustments varied with the duration of unemployment of the family head (see Table 11). Although the most prevalent types of adjustments, even for the very short-term unemployed, were decreasing savings, postponing purchases, borrowing money, piling up bills, and getting help from relatives, other types of adjustments began to play an increasingly significant role when unemployment lasted over a substantial period—moving to cheaper quarters, another member of the family becoming employed, and going on relief.[8] The rise in the proportion of families in which another member got a job tends to provide some support for the Woytinsky (213) "additional worker" hypothesis, although such adjustments do not usually take place on a large enough scale to bring about an increase in labor participation rates of women, young persons, or elderly persons (the groups from whom secondary workers are largely drawn) in recessions. In fact, there is some evidence that the reverse occurs (181, pp. 14-15, 30, and Chap. 11).[9]

These recent studies lend little support to a widely held impression that a large proportion of unemployed workers exhausting their insurance benefits seek public relief, at least in the relatively mild recessions that we have experienced since World War II. Whether so few families hit by unemployment resort to relief because of an aversion to "being on welfare," or exceedingly harsh eligibility conditions, or the virtual unavailability of assistance for the unemployed in some areas, is not revealed. What these studies do suggest is that the family—including the

[8]For additional evidence on the adjustments made by exhaustees, see 160.

[9]However, except for the substantial drop that occurred in the Great Depression of the thirties, Long regards the evidence for short-run changes in labor force participation rates in response to changes in employment conditions as largely inconclusive.

Table 11

PERCENT OF FAMILIES TAKING VARIOUS MEASURES TO MEET
UNEMPLOYMENT, BY DURATION OF UNEMPLOYMENT OF FAMILY
HEAD, UNITED STATES, 1958[a]

Measures taken	Duration of unemployment of head (in weeks)			
	1 to 4	5 to 13	14 to 26	27 and over
Decreased savings[b]	46	36	52	44
Postponed buying[b]	35	29	37	44
Borrowed money	17	19	28	22
Piled up bills	19	21	30	25
Got help from relatives	17	21	25	22
Moved to cheaper quarters	12	6	15	21
Other family member got job	4	7	7	15
Went on relief	—	2	7	8
Sold car or other durables	—	—	—	—
Other	2	4	12	5
None taken	27	14	7	6
Not ascertained	5	7	4	8
Average number of measures taken[c]	1.60	1.56	2.22	2.24
Number of cases				
June and October surveys	59	126	118	63
October only	26	58	60	34

[a]The data are based on nationwide surveys conducted by the Survey
Research Center of the University of Michigan in June and October,
1958. The table includes only those families where the head experienced
some unemployment. Except where otherwise noted, data from the June
and October surveys are combined.

[b]These measures were not specifically asked about in June; therefore, percentages in these categories are based only on October data.

[c]In computing the average number of measures, it was assumed that
the not-ascertained cases took, on the average, as many measures as
families for whom information was available.

Source: W. J. Cohen, William Haber, and Eva Mueller, *The Impact of
Unemployment in the 1958 Recession* (Ann Arbor, Institute of Labor and
Industrial Relations, University of Michigan and Wayne State Univer-
sity, 1960), p. 40.

extended family—continues to function as a unit in adjusting to
economic vicissitude in many instances, although it is probably
true that it performs this role less effectively than in earlier

periods. Here, however, is another example of our need for more adequate estimates of the social costs involved in unemployment. To the extent that families of the unemployed *and* their relatives dip into their savings, what is the effect of such adjustments over the life cycle, particularly for those employed in occupations and industries in which repeated spells of unemployment are prevalent? What is the effect on the education of children reared in such families, and how much would be saved in relief costs if unemployment benefit provisions were somewhat more liberal?

Over-all restoration of wage loss. What proportion of the aggregate wage loss associated with unemployment is restored through unemployment compensation? Lester's estimates (176 and 177) for the period from 1948 to 1960 provide the most detailed data bearing on this question that have been developed thus far.[10] On the average, over this 13-year period, unemployment benefits under the regular (state and railroad) public insurance programs compensated for about 20 percent of the wage and salary loss from total unemployment. If partial unemployment is included, the rate of compensation is reduced to 15 percent. However, if payments under all public programs providing unemployment benefits are taken into account, including the federal programs for servicemen and ex-servicemen and for temporary extension of benefits, the rates of compensation are raised to 23 percent for total unemployment and 18 percent for partial unemployment.

Lester also found that although the compensation rate tended to fluctuate over the business cycle it displayed a horizontal trend over the entire period, despite some expansion in coverage and increases in benefit duration. Apparently, the impact of expanded coverage and longer duration of benefits was offset by other factors—the increase in long-term unemployment and in part-year and part-time unemployment, the increase in the number

---

[10]His findings are, on the whole, consistent with those of other investigators, although, as he points out, significant differences may arise because of differences in the way wages are defined (whether gross earnings or net take-home pay are used) and in the method of measuring wage loss. See, also, 71, pp. 213-17; 152, and 195.

of new entrants to the labor force (with no rights to unemployment benefits), and the lag of increases in benefit ceilings behind wage increases. [11]

Over the entire course of a recession, recession-caused unemployment is compensated for at a rate no higher than the average compensation rate for all types of unemployment—seasonal, frictional, and technological, as well as cyclical. Yet, Lester argues (177, p. 19), a good case can be made for compensating recession unemployment at a higher rate than nonrecession unemployment. Variations in average rates of compensation for recession-caused unemployment among 16 selected states, moreover, were exceedingly wide (176, p. 358), ranging in the 1957-58 recession from lows of 6.2 percent and 9.7 percent in South Carolina and Michigan, respectively, to highs of 22.8 percent and 22.5 percent in New York and California.

There have been no comparable studies undertaken in other countries, so far as I am aware. However, the results would be likely to vary a great deal from country to country because of wide differences in coverage, benefit formulas, and duration provisions. Ribas (79, p. 33) shows that among seven European countries (the six Common Market countries and the United Kingdom), monthly unemployment benefits payable to a married iron and steel worker with two dependent children ranged from 19.3 percent and 36.7 percent of average gross monthly wages in Italy and the United Kingdom, respectively, at one end of the scale, to 55.8 percent and 79.8 percent in Luxembourg and The Netherlands at the other. [12]

COUNTERCYCLICAL EFFECTS

Unemployment insurance is generally regarded by economists as one of the most important "automatic stabilizers," along with

[11]Lester also suggests that some tightening of benefit disqualifications may have played a role.

[12]It should be noted that the systems in effect in France and Luxembourg are unemployment assistance schemes, imposing a needs test, rather than unemployment insurance. For information on unemployment compensation abroad, see 86 and 207. For a detailed, recent account of unemployment insurance provisions, as well as unemployment assistance and related programs, in the Common Market countries, see 190.

personal and corporate income taxes, undistributed corporate profits, and other transfer payments. Countercyclical effects operate automatically in these cases, at least theoretically, because net withdrawals from personal disposable income tend to increase during an upswing and to decline, or be replaced by net contributions to disposable income, in a recession, without the need for the government to take any action.

For purposes of analyzing the countercyclical effects of unemployment insurance, estimates of the percentage of wage loss restored in depressions are of interest, but we need to pay particular attention to changes in the *relationship* between total receipts and total benefit payments over the cycle. Lester's data (177, pp. 22-23) indicate that net contributions to disposable income in depressions have, particularly in recent years, been much more impressive than any net withdrawals during upswings. Following the 1957 downturn in business activity, for example, state benefit payments consistently exceeded state tax receipts from the third quarter of 1957 through the first quarter of 1959, with total benefits exceeding total receipts by nearly $2.5 billion over the period. However, for various reasons, state tax receipts exceeded state benefit payments in only three of the five generally prosperous quarters from the second quarter of 1959 through the second quarter of 1960, and for this five-quarter period as a whole benefit payments exceeded tax receipts by $67.7 million. The record was not significantly more impressive in the 1954-57 upswing, whereas in the 1950-53 upswing quarterly revenues consistently exceeded benefit payments.

It is true that the average unemployment rate was somewhat higher in the 1954-57 upswing, and decidedly higher in the 1958-60 upswing, than in 1950-53. However, if the system is to operate effectively in a countercyclical manner, tax rates must be maintained at high enough levels to bring in revenues that substantially exceed benefit payments in upswings. As we shall see, when we consider the financing of unemployment insurance, although many of the states have increased their tax rates, particularly since 1958, there has been considerable reluctance to raise taxes commensurately with benefit liabilities. Furthermore, as

Lester points out, the fact that the taxable earnings base has been held at its original level of $3,000 a year per worker in the great majority of states, despite the pronounced increase in earnings in the last two decades, has meant that increases in total earnings during upswings have been by no means fully reflected in increased tax revenues. [13] Finally, many state laws require an automatic shift to a lower tax schedule if the balance in the state fund rises to a certain level (in relation to taxable payrolls) or a shift to a higher tax schedule if the balance deteriorates, with the result that there is a tendency for tax rates to be lowered in upswings and increased in downswings.

Thus, if the effectiveness of the unemployment insurance system as an automatic stabilizer were to be maximized, state financing policies and practices would have to be changed in a number of ways, quite apart from any changes that might be considered in coverage or the benefit structure.

How does unemployment insurance compare with other automatic stabilizers in its countercyclical effects? Recent studies of the impact of automatic stabilizers by economists, which have already been mentioned in our discussion of OASDI, show that the unemployment insurance system has operated in a fairly consistent countercyclical matter, but that its relative impact as an automatic stabilizer has been far greater in recessions than in upswings. Clement (7, p. 60) estimates, for example, that on the average in the three postwar upswings (1948, 1949-53, and 1954-57), increases in unemployment insurance contributions and decreases in benefit payments together amounted to only 1.6 percent of national income changes, whereas the combined impact of all the automatic stabilizers which he analyzed amounted to 27.8 percent of national income changes. In two postwar downswings (1949 and 1953-54), however, changes (in the opposite direction) in unemployment insurance contributions and benefits amounted to 27.9 percent of national income changes, while the combined

[13]In addition, those employers who have a large proportion of workers earning more than $3,000 a year meet a substantial proportion of their tax liabilities in the first two quarters of the year, and, as a result, tax payments tend to fall off sharply in the third and fourth quarters.

impact of his stabilizers represented 51.3 percent. It was the increase in benefit payments in recessions, amounting to 26.2 percent of the decline in the national income, rather than the decline in payroll tax revenues, which was particularly significant.

In their recent attempt to analyze the effects of automatic stabilizers in various hypothetical recessions of differing degrees of severity, Duesenberry, Eckstein, and Fromm (13, p. 765) developed, among other things, an estimate of the effect of strengthening the unemployment insurance system. On the basis of two alternative models of a relatively severe recession, they estimated that increasing unemployment benefit payments by 50 percent (without changing contribution rates) would increase transfer payments during the recession by $2.4 billion, and reduce the estimated decline in GNP, from peak to trough, from $34 billion to $32 billion. They pointed out that with benefits no more than a third of average weekly wages a 50 percent increase would still leave benefits below one-half of wages. However, the countercyclical impact of such a change would clearly, on the basis of their estimates, be quite modest.

> While unemployment insurance is a perfect stabilizer insofar as it turns itself on and off with very little time lag and increases with the amount of decline that the economy has experienced, the total payments involved are simply too small, even after the policy change. Also, the inventory movements which constitute a large part of the changes in GNP are affected only by 0.4 billion by this policy. The experiments suggest, in summary, that the stability of the economy is somewhat improved by higher unemployment benefits but that this measure alone will leave the system quite unstable.

Clearly, there is room for further analysis of these questions, particularly since most of the studies of automatic stabilizers have treated unemployment insurance simply as one of a number of stabilizers and have not given close attention to the operation of the system, with a view to determining how its countercyclical effectiveness might be enhanced by various types of changes in coverage, benefit provisions, and financing.

WAGE EFFECTS

The jobless worker who is eligible for unemployment benefits need not take the first job that comes along, regardless of its skill or pay level. The Federal Unemployment Tax Act provides that he shall not be forced, as a condition for receipt of benefits, to accept wages below those prevailing for similar work in the locality. Nor may he be forced to resign from a union or to refrain from joining a union as a condition of employment. Beyond this, the policies in effect in most states permit him to hold out for work in his customary occupation for a reasonable length of time. However, if his unemployment continues for a considerable period, and prospects of reemployment in his usual occupation appear quite unfavorable, the state agency may sooner or later insist that he accept less skilled work or run the risk of disqualification for refusal of "suitable work." Clearly, his capacity to stick to a reservation price close to his previous level of earnings will depend to a considerable extent on how the state agency interprets suitable work (140 and 169).

In general, however, there is little question that unemployment insurance tends to increase a jobless worker's reservation price, i.e., the lowest wage at which he will accept employment (56, p. 75). Clearly, its precise effect is likely to depend to a considerable extent on the relationship between benefit levels and wage levels. The higher the ratio of benefits to wages, the higher the reservation price of an unemployed worker will tend to be, and, since the benefit-wage ratio under our benefit structure and those of many other countries tends to be higher for relatively low-paid workers than those with larger earnings, the impact of unemployment insurance on prevailing wages, like that of minimum wage laws, is likely to be particularly significant at the lower end of the wage scale.

> Insofar as the benefit level does restrict the available labor supply for low-paying or low-grade work, it is a force exerting pressure for improvement in the wages, work conditions, or promotion prospects for such jobs .... [68, p. 305]

Indeed, unemployment insurance has probably had some impact even on the supply of labor and the wage level in occupations, such as farm laborer, which are not covered by the system. The tendency of unemployed urban workers to seek farm work in recessions has probably been less pronounced in recent decades than in earlier periods (168) when jobless benefits were unavailable, although the impact of this factor on farm wage rates has undoubtedly been offset, at least to some extent, by the importation of Mexican laborers. [14]

Through its effect on the reservation price of the jobless worker, unemployment insurance tends to provide support for union efforts to bargain for wage increases and enforce union rates. Recognition of the importance of this influence helps to explain the vigor of organized labor's drive for higher benefits and longer duration, as well as the determined resistance of employer groups to liberalization of benefit provisions. [15]

It seems likely, also, that unemployment insurance has played a role, along with greater union strength, the impact of

[14]It should be noted that if we take account of the effect of employer-financed supplemental unemployment benefit systems (SUB plans) in certain industries we must qualify, to some extent, our statement that the benefit-wage ratio is more favorable for low earners, since the purpose of these plans, in general, is to bring total unemployment benefits (public benefits plus SUB payments) for all workers up to 65 percent of the individual's take-home pay. For a description of these plans, which are found in the automobile, steel, rubber, electrical, and a few other industries, see 169, pp. 69-73. There have been a number of improvements in some of these plans in the last few years. The Chrysler plan, for example, now provides for supplementation up to 65 percent of *gross,* rather than *take-home,* pay, plus $1.50 per dependent up to a maximum of four dependents, with a maximum weekly SUB payment of $40 for hourly workers and $50 for salaried workers. The maximum duration of SUB payments is 52 weeks. For further details, see 159.

[15]Moreover, the early attempts of unions, particularly in a number of European countries, to establish voluntary unemployment benefit funds, and their later struggle for compulsory systems were motivated, at least in part, by recognition of this relationship. Voluntary union-sponsored plans were less prevalent in the United States, and it was not until 1932 that the American Federation of Labor decided to support the establishment of a public unemployment insurance system. For a good account of the shift in the AFL position under the impact of the Great Depression, see 146, pp. 347-54.

other automatic stabilizers, and government full-employment policies, in preventing wage declines in mild recessions.[16] Schultze (197, pp. 61-62) has shown that although there has been a tendency toward an inverse relationship between annual percentage changes in wages and average annual unemployment rates, wage increases occurring at given unemployment levels tended to be considerably more pronounced in 1947-58 than in 1900-13.

> A 4 percent unemployment rate roughly implied a 3 percent wage increase in the earlier period, whereas it seems to imply an annual increase of some 5 percent in the postwar period....However, the relationship between wage rates and unemployment breaks down once unemployment falls below 5 percent.

In a more recent article, France (164), shows that differences in wage behavior between the "essentially non-union pre-World War I era" and the 1953-59 period showed up chiefly in recessions.[17] Along with other recent analysts of these relationships, France appears to attribute the increased tendency of wages to rise in recession years to the growth of collective bargaining and does not discuss the possible influence of unemployment insur-

[16]Data prepared by the National Bureau of Economic Research indicate that there was a tendency for average hourly earnings in manufacturing to continue rising in the early phases of downswings in the twenties but to decline significantly in the late stages of downswings, whereas in the postwar period average hourly earnings have tended to level off after the business peak but to show no significant decline thereafter. See 22, p. 286, for charts showing National Bureau "reference-cycle" patterns.

[17]In the recession years of 1954 and 1958, wages rose more than 3 percent, whereas in recession years during the first decade of the present century wage changes ranged from +1.2 percent to −1.4 percent. France's article is also a useful source for reference to the rapidly growing literature on the relationships between wage changes, price changes, and unemployment rates. One of the best known and frequently cited of these studies is 187. Although this study maintained that the relationship between wage changes, the unemployment rate, and the rate of change of unemployment had remained remarkably stable over a period of almost a hundred years, this conclusion has more recently been disputed. See, for example, 180.

ance. However, a British study published in the thirties (212) indicated that unemployment insurance had been considerably less influential than other factors in explaining changes in wage behavior. This study showed that although British wages were relatively flexible from 1850 to 1880 there was already considerable rigidity by the eighties and nineties, that the increasing ability of the workers to oppose wage reductions was attributable to the growing acceptance of collective bargaining and of the concept of a decent standard of living, and that unemployment insurance (first introduced in Britain in 1911 on a very limited scale and substantially expanded in the twenties) had little effect on the bargaining power of the unions because benefits were so low that they were seldom an attractive alternative to wages.

Although it is generally assumed that whatever influence unemployment insurance has on wage levels is favorable either to wage increases or greater wage rigidity in recessions, there arc certain situations in which the availability of unemployment benefits may exert a depressing effect on wages. There is some evidence that seasonal employers "use unemployment benefits as a means of holding from year to year a reserve of workers who may wish only part-year work if they can supplement their wage income with unemployment benefits." Thus, the system "may, in effect, provide a sort of subsidy that permits low-wage employers to attract and hold labor by offering a combination of pay and benefits" (177, p. 50). If this is true for some seasonal employers, it is probably also true for some employers using casual or intermittent labor.

EFFECTS ON LABOR MOBILITY

In recent years, in an environment of growing concern over the persistence of an unsatisfactorily high unemployment rate, the charge has been made with increasing frequency, by economists and others, that unemployment insurance interferes unduly with labor mobility. Although this accusation is undoubtedly valid in some situations, those who make this type of charge often fail to recognize that in the interests of preservation of work skills the unemployment insurance system *should* function in such a way as to protect the jobless worker from the necessity of accepting the first job that comes along, if it is substantially below his prcvious skill level. Such critics also frequently display ignorance of the conclusions that can be drawn from the vast and growing literature on labor mobility.

In analyzing the impact of unemployment insurance on labor mobility, it is important to distinguish between job mobility, on the one hand, and occupational, industrial, and geographical mobility, on the other. We are really concerned with two questions, although they are somewhat interrelated. To what extent do jobless workers postpone vigorous efforts to obtain reemployment as long as they are eligible for unemployment benefits? And to what extent does the system interfere with desirable interoccupational, interindustrial, and interarea shifts?

Job mobility. So far as the first question is concerned, there is relatively little evidence that unemployed workers, particularly primary wage-earners with firm attachments to the labor force, tend to postpone vigorous efforts to obtain reemployment when employment opportunities are favorable. The fact that in prosperous years only about a fifth of all beneficiaries exhaust their benefits, as compared with an appreciably higher ratio in recession years, provides evidence that if jobs are available relatively few jobless workers are content to receive benefits as long as they are eligible instead of going back to work.[18] Another type of evidence is provided by some of the local labor market studies that have been conducted in periods when employment opportunities were relatively favorable. Particularly pertinent was a study of the experience of displaced workers following the closing of an International Harvester Company plant in Auburn, New York (138, p. 157). In this situation, "enough new job openings developed within 6 months of the Harvester shutdown so that few displaced workers exhausted their benefits. Those who were unemployed for more than 26 weeks were older workers without highly developed skills."

On the other hand, there appears to be some tendency for

[18]For data on the total number of beneficiaries and the number who exhaust benefits each year, see 221, September, 1961, p. 7.

workers with less firm attachments to the labor force to collect unemployment benefits without making vigorous efforts to obtain other jobs. Although such persons apparently constitute a fairly small minority of all beneficiaries, it is not easy to determine from the available data just how prevalent these practices may be. A study of benefit exhaustions conducted in 1956, a year of relatively favorable employment opportunities, indicated that women constituted a higher proportion of exhaustees (42 percent) than of all claimants (36 percent). Furthermore, women were more likely than men to have withdrawn from the labor force two or four months after exhaustion of their benefit rights. Workers aged 65 or over were also particularly likely to have withdrawn (162, pp. 5-6).

There is also evidence that abuse of the unemployment insurance system is more prevalent among married women with loose attachments to the labor force and intermittent workers, as well as among lower-income and less educated workers, than among other groups. But Father Becker's authoritative and careful study of this problem (145) indicated that in "normal" times, at least in New York State, not more than 1 to 2 percent of benefits went to persons who abused the system. It also provided considerable evidence that abuse could be held to minimal proportions through careful and effective administration.

As Wilcock (211) and Lester (177, Chap. 4) have recently pointed out, forces on both the demand and supply sides of the labor market are leading to an increase in the relative proportion of persons with part-time and intermittent patterns of work. Comparatively rapid growth of the trade and service industries, on the one hand, has created more opportunities for such work, while the influx of married women into the labor force, the prolongation of schooling, and the trend toward earlier retirement from one's regular job have all tended to bring about an increase in the supply of workers who are interested in part-time or intermittent work.

Wilcock suggests that these trends indicate a need for careful study of the possibility of discriminating between primary and secondary workers in our unemployment insurance provisions. He calls attention, particularly, to Altman's earlier recommendation

(140, p. 237) that persons with no dependents (a large majority of women workers) should be required to have larger total earnings or more weeks of employment in the base period than persons with dependents. Father Becker, in his recent analysis of the adequacy of unemployment benefits (144), suggests the desirability of modifying the benefit formula to provide either 1) a larger proportion of previous wages for beneficiaries with dependents or 2) higher maximum benefits for such beneficiaries.

Clearly, there are a number of different ways in which the system could be amended to improve the relative position of primary versus secondary workers, not all of them involving discrimination. Some of the possibilities will be discussed more fully at a later stage, but the issue is raised here to bring out the point that the answer does not lie solely in more vigorous attempts to enforce "seek work" requirements or to "crack down" on violators.

Occupational, industrial, and geographical mobility. There is a wealth of evidence that the American labor force is extraordinarily adaptable and that the proportion of workers who experience interoccupational, interindustrial, or interarea shifts in the course of a year or a decade is remarkably high. Mobility studies also indicate clearly that the propensity to make such changes varies with age, education, occupation, and other factors.

Although any attempt to review the literature on labor mobility would be well beyond the scope of this study, several points are particularly important in the present context (141, 185, and 186). The frequency of shifts of all types tends to rise in periods of expanding employment opportunities and to decline in periods when labor market conditions are less favorable. Mobility often entails costs—the costs of acquiring a new skill, of giving up pension or seniority rights, of moving to a new area—and such costs can be more readily incurred when the prospects for improving one's position through an appropriate shift are favorable. Perhaps particularly important is the fact that a home can often be readily sold at a favorable price by a worker who wishes to move in prosperous periods, but the market for homes will tend to be less advantageous in a recession and highly unfavorable in a depressed area.

Secondly, there are many institutional barriers to labor mobility, of which unemployment insurance is only one. Discriminatory hiring practices, union control of referral procedures in certain industries, seniority and pension rights, and supplemental unemployment benefit plans all tend to interfere with mobility. But at least one recent study (196) has cast considerable doubt on the widely held view that institutional changes have resulted in a decline in mobility rates as compared with earlier periods, while the annual mobility surveys conducted by the U. S. Bureau of the Census (216) in the postwar period do not reveal any downward trend in the proportion of the population involved in either intercounty or interstate shifts in residence between 1947 and 1960.

However, relatively few studies have been designed to shed much light on the impact of unemployment insurance per se, on occupational, industrial, and geographical mobility. Altman's study (140) yields a good deal of information on the principles which have been applied in interpreting the "availability" and "refusal of suitable work" provisions, but there is a need for community surveys which would be specifically designed to analyze the relationship between policies followed in administering unemployment insurance and the types of job shifts that occur under varying labor market conditions.

Nevertheless, it has become increasingly clear that however inclined state agencies administering unemployment insurance may have been to encourage appropriate occupational, industrial, or geographical shifts, they have had relatively few tools at their disposal to further this purpose, particularly as compared with their counterparts in some of the countries of western Europe. The fact that most job placements occur through channels other than the public employment service represents a serious handicap (171). Until recently, moreover, jobless workers who were unavailable for work because they were enrolled in training or retraining programs would have been declared ineligible for benefits in practically all the states, and, although there has been a trend toward modifying these provisions to permit the payment of extended or regular benefits to claimants enrolled in approved training programs, only 11 jurisdictions had provisions permitting such payments in 1961 (194, p. 14). Another handicap has been the weakness or complete absence of any coordination between the public employment service, on the one hand, and the various public and private agencies involved in sponsoring training programs on the other—employer on-the-job training programs, apprenticeship programs, adult education courses, and numerous others. Finally, there have been no special provisions for retraining or relocation allowances, as in many European countries.

Now much of this is changing. And yet the recent measures to stimulate retraining raise a host of questions. To what extent will retraining aid in getting jobless workers back to work in the absence of a marked increase in the rate of expansion of employment opportunities? How well equipped are we to identify the occupations for which workers should be retrained? To what extent will retraining and reemployment be hampered, as in the Armour situation (189), by the fact that a large proportion of laid-off workers who do not readily obtain reemployment are, because of lack of education or for other reasons, poorly qualified for retraining?[19] To what extent should emphasis be placed on stimulating the location of industry in depressed areas versus encouraging the movement of unemployed workers out of such areas? Will retraining allowances be high enough and available long enough to provide adequate inducement to jobless workers to enter and complete training programs? In this connection, what administrative complications will result from the differing provisions in the Area Redevelopment Act of 1961, the Manpower Development and Training Act of 1962, and the adjustment assistance features of the Trade Expansion Act?

[19]In this context, Neil Chamberlain's recent suggestion that workers be permitted to accumulate years of potential educational benefits to facilitate periodic reeducation during the course of their working lives, much as they now accumulate unemployment or retirement benefits, is of considerable interest. See 167.

Under the Area Redevelopment Act (193), retraining allowances equal average weekly unemployment benefits in each state and may be paid for periods up to 16 weeks. The Manpower Development and Training Act (191) permits the payment of training allowances equal to the average unemployment compensation rate in each state, or to the worker's own benefit rate if he is eligible for compensation at a rate above the average, for periods up to 52 weeks. Travel and subsistence allowances are also provided if training is available in facilities that are not within commuting distance from the trainee's residence.

The Trade Expansion Act of 1962 (203) provides for the payment of readjustment allowances to workers who have been totally or partially separated from a firm that has been found to have been adversely affected by tariff concessions. The weekly readjustment allowance for a totally unemployed worker will be equal to either 1) 65 percent of the worker's average weekly wage or 2) 65 percent of the national average weekly wage in manufacturing, whichever is less. The allowances are payable for a maximum period of 52 weeks, except that if the adversely affected worker is participating in approved training he may receive an additional 26 weeks of allowances to assist him in completing his training. If the worker is age 60 or older, he may receive an additional 13 weeks of allowances, i.e., without training, a maximum of 65 weeks of allowances. The act also provides subsistence and transportation allowances similar to those under the MDTA program. Significantly, also, unlike the other two acts, it provides for the payment of relocation allowances to unemployed heads of families who have no reasonable prospects for suitable reemployment locally and who have obtained or been offered a job in another area.

Sooner or later, if we are to avoid serious inequities among individuals who become unemployed under differing circumstances, such policies will have to be made more uniform and more closely integrated with the federal-state unemployment insurance system. This may well require greater federal participation in the financing of unemployment insurance. There are also strong arguments for making relocation allowances more generally available under conditions similar to those set forth in the Trade Expansion Act.

CRITERIA FOR BENEFIT LEVELS

How high should unemployment benefits be? Particularly in a short-term benefit program such as unemployment insurance, there is much to be said for earnings-related benefits as opposed to flat benefits, since the latter must be geared to earnings at the bottom of the wage scale if they are not to provide a disincentive for low earners to return to work, and will thus be likely to require drastic cuts in expenditures on the part of jobless workers accustomed to higher earnings. But even among countries with earnings-related benefits, there are wide differences in the benefit-wage ratio.

The recommendation of President Roosevelt's Committee on Economic Security for benefits equaling 50 percent of weekly wages (78), which was followed in most of the original state laws, was influenced partly by study of European systems and partly by actuarial estimates (based on highly inadequate unemployment data for the 1920s) which indicated that it would require a 3 percent payroll tax—the highest tax it was felt the economy could stand at the time—to provide benefits at the 50 percent level for a maximum period of 15 weeks and with a benefit ceiling of $15. However, despite liberalization of benefit and duration provisions, costs have been far below 3 percent throughout most of the period since the laws were first enacted, because unemployment rates have been considerably lower than was anticipated and changes in benefit ceilings have lagged behind wage increases (see Table 12). Nevertheless, the 50 percent benefit standard has been supported by successive administrations and is embodied in the Kennedy Administration's 1961 proposals for permanent revision of the unemployment insurance system, including federally imposed benefit standards. The recommendations which the President submitted to Congress in June 1961 (156) would, among other things, require the states to provide benefits equal to 50 percent of a worker's average weekly wage up to a benefit ceiling which would be raised, in a series of

Table 12

UNEMPLOYMENT INSURANCE BENEFIT COSTS, AS PERCENT OF TAXABLE WAGES, UNITED STATES AND 10 LARGEST STATES, 1945–61

State	1945	1946	1947	1948	1949	1950	1951	1952	1953	1954	1955	1956	1957	1958	1959	1960	1961
United States	0.8	0.7	1.1	1.0	2.3	1.7	0.9	1.1	1.0	2.1	1.4	1.3	1.5	3.2	2.0	2.3	2.9
California	1.1	2.8	2.1	2.2	4.0	2.7	1.2	1.2	1.1	1.6	1.1	0.9	1.4	3.0	1.8	3.0	3.4
Illinois	0.8	1.6	0.8	0.8	1.8	1.5	0.9	0.8	0.7	1.9	1.1	0.8	1.0	2.8	1.6	1.7	2.3
Massachusetts	0.6	1.5	1.7	1.5	3.7	2.3	1.3	1.6	1.1	2.0	1.4	1.1	1.8	3.1	2.1	2.8	3.2
Michigan	2.3	2.3	0.8	0.8	1.9	1.1	1.0	1.2	0.7	2.8	1.2	2.6	2.2	6.3	2.5	2.6	4.1
New Jersey	1.4	2.8	1.8	1.5	2.8	1.9	1.2	1.3	1.4	2.9	2.3	2.3	2.7	4.3	2.8	2.8	3.2
New York	0.7	2.1	1.7	1.7	3.3	2.7	1.6	1.5	1.4	2.3	1.7	1.5	1.7	3.5	2.8	2.6	3.2
North Carolina	0.2	0.5	0.5	0.5	1.6	1.2	1.1	1.2	1.2	2.3	1.4	1.3	1.6	2.4	1.4	1.5	2.0
Ohio	0.5	1.2	0.4	0.4	1.5	1.4	0.4	0.5	0.5	1.9	0.9	0.8	1.1	3.9	1.7	2.8	3.8
Pennsylvania	0.5	1.6	0.9	0.6	2.0	1.5	0.8	1.3	1.2	3.3	2.2	1.9	2.2	4.7	3.1	3.1	4.2
Texas	0.2	0.7	0.3	0.2	0.4	0.5	0.2	0.2	0.3	0.6	0.4	0.5	0.7	1.5	1.1	1.2	1.3

Source: *The Labor Market and Employment Security.*

steps, to two-thirds of the average weekly wage in each state by 1968.

Although a good many economists have recommended federally imposed benefit standards in recent years, there is anything but unanimity on how high benefits ought to be. Mrs. Burns (56, pp. 60 and 79) points out that the differential between benefits and earnings is expected to operate as a "bait to encourage people to prefer work and the higher income that can thus be secured," but maintains that there has been relatively little research of a kind that would assist in policy determination on this and related issues. Lester (68, p. 301) comments that the use of the differential rests on the assumption that one can "draw up some kind of schedule of propensity for benefits in relation to the size of the differential between benefit and normal pay. . . . as the differential disappeared,, the propensity, and hence the number of workers preferring a benefit status would increase." However, he goes on to express considerable skepticism about the possibilities of developing such a schedule from empirical data and, in the concluding section of his recent book (177, p. 127) recommends that the federal act should be amended to require the states to maintain a maximum weekly benefit equal to a certain percentage (say 60 percent) of the average weekly wage in the state, so that most beneficiaries would receive at least half of their gross wage.[20]

By far the boldest and most far-reaching recommendation on benefit levels made by an economist in recent years is Galbraith's proposal (18, pp. 292-307) for "cyclically graduated compensation" (CGC). Galbraith argues that benefits need not represent a high proportion of lost earnings when the economy is operating at close to full employment, since at such times unemployed workers can easily achieve reemployment and low bene-

[20] Alternatively, he suggests, the state might be required to adopt a less mechanical standard under which it would have to certify that two-thirds of its totally unemployed beneficiaries were receiving 50 percent of their average weekly earnings in the base period.

These recommendations represent a slight modification of earlier recommendations made jointly by Lester and J. Douglas Brown to the House Ways and Means Committee. See 178.

fits do not, therefore, cause much hardship. Higher benefit levels, under such conditions, moreover, are subject to the objection that they may contribute to inflationary pressures. "If unemployment is a financially attractive alternative to employment, the bargaining position, both of individual workers and of unions, will be increased" (p. 296).

When the economy is not operating at close to full employment, however, "conditions are almost exactly reversed" (p. 297). Efforts to achieve reemployment will be unavailing as long as there is an insufficiency of aggregate demand (pp. 297-98), and high compensation rates will therefore not interfere with reemployment. Nor, so long as "the capacity of the economy and the labor force are not being fully used," will high compensation rates add to inflationary pressures, but they will have the great advantage of adding to income and consumer demand.

Specifically, Galbraith proposes federally financed supplementary benefits which would become payable when total unemployment rose above the level associated with full employment conditions. The amount of the supplement would be directly related to the severity of unemployment and would rise to a maximum of four-fifths of the difference between the claimant's ordinary benefit under his state system and his previous wage.[21] Ordinary benefits would continue to be paid by the states, as at present, but there should be federal standards affecting the level of benefits.

My own view is that the 50 percent standard is essentially arbitrary and that economists could make a significant contribution to the development of more carefully framed criteria for benefit levels, whether cyclically graduated or not, through appropriate research efforts. Here, again, as in connection with OASDI, I believe that carefully designed and executed cross-national studies might shed some light on the impact of various

---

[21]However one views the Galbraith proposal, a question might well be raised as to whether maximum supplementary benefits should be related to gross earnings or to take-home pay. Galbraith does not deal with this question, although his discussion implies that he is thinking in terms of gross earnings.

benefit-wage ratios on incentives to work. Such studies could also provide information on the advantages and disadvantages of various alternative methods of providing more adequate benefits for jobless heads of families than for single beneficiaries or secondary workers, since foreign systems not only almost invariably provide dependents' benefits but also offer a good many illustrations of various other methods of giving an advantage to primary earners or to persons with records of continuous attachment to the labor force.

THE ISSUE OF BENEFIT DURATION

There is general agreement that there must be definite limits on the duration of benefits in an unemployment insurance system which provides benefits as a matter of right to jobless workers who have "earned" this right through contributions that have been made on their behalf. Britain's unfortunate experience with extended and "transitional" benefits in the twenties (149) is often cited as a glaring example of the way in which an insurance system tends to break down if an attempt is made to meet a problem of persistently high unemployment through repeated liberalization of duration provisions.

But have we found a satisfactory answer to the issue of benefit duration? Although the states have liberalized their duration provisions, and the great majority now permit payment of benefits up to 26 weeks or more, the threat of widespread exhaustion of benefits in both the 1957-58 and 1960-61 recessions led the federal government to step in with temporary legislation providing for extended benefits. Under the 1961 Administration proposals for revision of the system, moreover, federally financed extended benefits would become a permanent feature. Exhaustees would be entitled to extended benefits for a period 50 percent longer than the state permitted up to a maximum extension of 13 weeks, but, except in recession periods when the usual state eligibility conditions would apply, an exhaustee would have to show that he had worked at least 78 weeks in the last three years and at least 13 weeks in each year of this three-year period (156 and 199).

This legislation would have the effect of providing for maximum duration of 39 weeks in a large percentage of cases. To what extent is this an arbitrary answer, and is there a rational basis for resisting further pressure for a longer maximum if long-term unemployment continues to be a problem?

As Mrs. Burns pointed out over a quarter of a century ago (150), British and German experience indicated that the extent of pressure to extend unemployment insurance benefits depends on the adequacy of the alternative kinds of relief available. Only when these countries took steps to make reasonably adequate public assistance payments available to exhaustees were they able to overcome pressure to provide greatly extended unemployment insurance benefits. More recently (56, pp. 112-17), she has also discussed at some length the pros and cons of extending the duration of unemployment insurance versus increasing expenditures on public works as a means of meeting the type of unemployment problem that might be encountered in a severe recession.

Thus, the issue of duration of unemployment insurance benefits cannot be adequately considered without paying some attention to the public assistance system and other public policies for dealing with long-term unemployment. In this country, unlike many countries in western Europe and the British Commonwealth, we do not have a national program of unemployment assistance. Under the public assistance titles of the Social Security Act, federal grants-in-aid are provided to the states for the so-called categorical aids—old-age assistance, aid to the blind, aid to dependent children (normally available only if at least one parent is disabled or absent from the home, but extended temporarily to children of unemployed workers under legislation enacted in 1961 and 1962), aid to the permanently and totally disabled, and the new program of medical aid to the aged (adopted under the Kerr-Mills Act of 1960). But no federal funds are available for general relief, which is usually administered by the counties and often financed exclusively by the counties without state support. Eligibility conditions are frequently harshly restrictive, monthly payments are generally considerably below those available in the categorical aid programs, and, in a good many parts of the

country, regulations and policies are such as to effectively shut
off any relief to the unemployed.[22]

Thus, in the light of this background, the 1961 federal legislation to extend unemployment benefits on a temporary basis and
the separately enacted program to provide federal matching funds
for extension of aid to dependent children to the children of jobless workers must be seen as two closely related steps to meet
a situation in which public assistance for the unemployed was
either absent or highly restrictive.

It was in recognition of these relationships that Lester included, along with his recommendations for changes in the unemployment insurance system, a proposal for establishing a federal
matching program on a 50-50 basis for general relief. On unemployment benefit duration, his recommendations agreed quite
closely with the Kennedy Administration proposals, discussed
above.

Galbraith believes (18, p. 301) that his proposed CGC payments plus normal benefits should be paid as long as unemployment is above specified levels, without any specific limit on
duration of benefits for individual unemployed workers, and with
the federal government footing the bill not only for CGC supplements but also for any extension of ordinary benefits beyond the
limits provided in the state law.

On the issue of benefit duration, as on that of benefit levels,
I would again urge more careful study of the experience of other
countries. Would there be advantages, for example, in moving
much farther than has thus far been proposed in the direction of
providing substantially extended duration of benefits for workers
with a record of steady attachment to the labor force in the preceding five or ten years, while strictly limiting it for workers who
can barely meet requirements for a minimum amount of employ-

[22]Robert Goodwin, Administrator of the U. S. Bureau of Employment
Security, speaking before the 1959 Conference of Employment Security
Agencies, noted (158) that 23 states had no general public assistance
available either to employable persons who are out of work or their
families. In the other states, he maintained, the means test was typically so severe that a person had to be practically destitute to be eligible for relief. See, also, 151 and 192.

ment or earnings in the preceding year, as is done under some foreign systems? Among other things, such an approach would give an advantage to older workers, primary wage-earners, and all those with steady attachments to the labor force, without specifically discriminating between primary and secondary workers.

FINANCING AND FEDERAL-STATE RELATIONSHIPS

The questions that need to be asked about the financing of unemployment insurance are similar to those that were asked in connection with OASDI, but with certain differences. In view of the decision that was made in 1935 to adopt a federal-state system of unemployment insurance, the question of the appropriate distribution of the financial burden between the federal and state governments is an important issue in this program and is inseparable from the question of the division of responsibility between the two levels of government for control of the system. Much of our previous discussion of OASDI financing, however, is relevant to unemployment insurance, and we shall concentrate attention on those questions that are particularly important in the financing of unemployment insurance rather than reconsider some of the issues that were discussed under OASDI.

The American system of financing unemployment insurance is unique. The tax-offset device through which the federal government induced the states to enact unemployment insurance laws is, of course, irrelevant in countries that do not have a federal form of government. But our exclusive reliance (except in a few states) on a payroll tax imposed on employers and our experience rating system are also not found elsewhere.[23] Most countries either have a tripartite scheme of financing, or, where the government subsidizes union-sponsored schemes which originated on a voluntary basis (the Ghent system), they rely on contributions from insured persons and the government.

[23]Yugoslavia, however, does rely on a payroll tax imposed on the state-owned enterprises. This pattern of financing social insurance is also followed in the countries of the Soviet bloc, but they do not have unemployment insurance systems. Italy and Spain rely exclusively on employer contributions, but they are not subject to experience rating (86).

Early controversies. The principle of experience rating was, as is well known, strongly advocated by John R. Commons and his followers at the University of Wisconsin. Commons had drafted the Wisconsin workmen's compensation law, which embodied the principle that the employer's contribution rate should vary directly with the accident record in his plant.[24] He became convinced that just as an employer might be induced to place increased emphasis on safety measures in order to reduce his workmen's compensation costs so he could be encouraged to make greater efforts to stabilize employment in his firm if this would result in a reduction in his unemployment insurance costs. Furthermore, the costs of unemployment compensation should in large part be a charge against specific firms and industries. Commons and his followers (170) objected to a pooled insurance fund on the ground that it would force industries with stable employment to subsidize those with seasonal or irregular employment. Following this principle, the so-called Wisconsin plan, which was embodied in the law adopted by that state in 1932, called for a separate "unemployment reserve" for each covered employer, from which benefits would be paid to any of his employees who became involuntarily unemployed.

The Wisconsin plan was opposed by many economists, some of whom favored the plan proposed by an Ohio commission in 1932, under which employer and employee contributions would be pooled in a single insurance fund, while others felt that nothing short of a national system, with tripartite financing modeled on the British approach, would meet the need (57, 60, 90, and 146, Chap. 15).

In the deliberations associated with the work of the Committee on Economic Security, by far the most heated controversy was over the question of an outright federal system versus a federal-state scheme under which the states would be induced to adopt their own laws either through a tax-offset device or some type of federal grant-in-aid program. The decision to recommend

---

[24]This principle is found in nearly all workmen's compensation laws and grew out of earlier private insurance practices relating to employer's liability rates in industrial accident insurance.

a federal-state system was influenced not merely by the political strength of the advocates of states' rights but also by the difficulty of resolving the controversy between the proponents of the Wisconsin plan and a pooled reserve system. Alvin H. Hansen (172), for example, decided, evidently somewhat reluctantly, to support a federal-state system, partly because he feared advocacy of a national system would prove abortive, and partly because he felt it would be desirable to permit the states to experiment with different types of systems.

This point of view was vigorously opposed by such economists as Eveline M. Burns (150) and Paul H. Douglas (now Senator Douglas) (161) who were highly critical of the federal-state approach, the tax-offset device, and experience rating. The reasons which they advanced in opposition to the proposed unemployment insurance provisions of the Social Security Act anticipated many of the difficulties that later arose under the federal-state system. Among the points which they emphasized were: 1) in the absence of federal standards affecting benefit provisions, there would be a tendency for the states to compete with each other to keep their costs down; 2) the possibilities of stabilizing employment through action by individual firms were greatly exaggerated; 3) the tax-offset provision would be a less effective device for ensuring adequate state systems than some type of federal grant-in-aid program under which grants could be withheld from states failing to comply with minimum standards of benefits and administration; and 4) the tax-offset scheme would tend to restrict not only present but future financing.

The subsequent controversy over experience rating. In subsequent years, the experience-rating aspect of unemployment compensation financing has been the particular target of criticism by many economists, although others have joined industry representatives in supporting the system (56, pp. 165ff.; and 173, 177, 179, 182, and 210).

At the heart of the attack on experience rating is the contention that most unemployment, particularly of the cyclical type, is attributable to forces beyond the control of the individual employer. Secondly, any savings he can make through a lower unemployment compensation tax rate are minimal compared with the payroll savings associated with laying off workers when business conditions call for it. Thirdly, since contributory tax rates vary substantially from firm to firm within industries as well as from industry to industry, the chances are strong that only those employers whose contributory rates are relatively low within their own industries will be able to pass the tax on to the consumer.[25] This difficulty of shifting the tax, it has been suggested, helps to explain the vigor of employer opposition to liberalizing amendments that would increase the costs of the system.

Moreover, partly because of the problem of interstate competition, the states are inhibited from burdening their high-cost employers with the full costs of unemployment compensation to their employees.[26] Finally, it has been argued, experience rating has tended to generate controversy over just how any given change in the tax structure should be distributed among low-cost and high-cost employers and has also tended to encourage a variety of devices for holding down charges against individual employer ac-

[25]The variability of the tax rates from year to year also inhibits shifting. Lester concludes that perhaps no more than a third of the unemployment compensation tax burden is shifted to the consumer. For other discussions of the problem of tax incidence, see 42, 56, pp. 160-71; and 65, Chaps. 15 and 17-20; and, for a recent analysis of the problem of price determination under tax rates that vary from firm to firm, 148, pp. 284-93.

[26]It is true that in recent years, maximum rates have been raised a good deal (see Appendix) and some states have imposed special penalty rates on employers with negative reserve accounts. But, in general, the increase in maximum rates has been chiefly attributable to the rise in average unemployment insurance costs.

It should be noted that data on variations in cost by industry tend to conceal the high-cost industries in broader industry groupings. Data relating to the ratio of benefits to taxable wages by fairly detailed industry groups in California in 1956 indicate that the ratio was 3 percent or more in the following industries: farms, agricultural and similar service establishments and forestry, 3.3 percent; fishing, 4.1 percent; food and kindred products, 3.3 percent, tobacco manufactures, 27.5 percent; apparel manufacturing, 3.0 percent; lumber and wood products (except furniture), 3.0 percent; nonclassifiable industries, 4.5 percent. (Covered workers on farms, it should be noted, include categories of employees other than farm laborers.) See 174.

counts.[27] Opposition to raising the earnings base, for example, comes in good part from employers with low unemployment insurance costs, whose steadily employed workers are likely to be earning more than $3,000 a year and who see the restrictive earnings base as a means of shifting more of the relative cost burden to employers whose workers are employed seasonally or intermittently and are likely to be earning less than $3,000 a year.

Finally, the fact that so many states have provisions under which a shift to a higher tax schedule automatically takes place when the balance in the fund falls below a certain point is, as we have seen, inconsistent with countercyclical principles of financing. However, this method of timing changes in tax rates is not a necessary feature of experience rating, as the policies followed in Wisconsin and Arizona indicate (see Appendix).

Present-day defenders of experience rating tend to place less emphasis than did Commons and his followers on its role in inducing employers to stabilize employment and more emphasis on its importance as a means of inducing the employer to "police" the system. They argue that experience rating provides employers with a strong inducement to exercise a close watch on all claims for compensation by their former employees and thus to play an important role in preventing abuse. It is also argued that certain practices, under which unemployment compensation becomes a kind of wage subsidy,[28] particularly in industries with seasonal or intermittent unemployment, would be even more prevalent in the absence of experience rating, since it is chiefly those employers whose unemployment compensation costs are not fully reflected in their contributory tax rates who engage in such practices (173, p. 105). Finally, the fact that experience

[27]The pressure for more stringent disqualification provisions, for example, has been partly motivated by this objective, as well as by a desire to restrict over-all costs, while the practice of "noncharging" (under which the costs of compensating jobless workers are not charged against individual employer accounts under stipulated conditions) is clearly an attempt to protect individual accounts at the expense of the system as a whole.

[28]Cf. above discussion.

rating gives employers a strong and direct interest in keeping down the costs of the system is considered essential as a counterbalance to the tendency of employee representatives to press vigorously for more liberal benefit provisions.

In spite of all the debate, we really have very little documented evidence on the impact of experience rating on the behavior of firms, nor do we have much information on whether the absence of experience rating in other countries is an obstacle to the prevention of abuse. Indeed, under the full employment conditions that have prevailed in a number of European countries in recent years, there have been almost no studies of any aspects of their unemployment compensation systems.

Federal-state financial relationships. In the last few years, high unemployment insurance costs have created a situation which has brought the issue of federal-state financing relationships to the forefront. Unemployment compensation costs vary greatly from state to state, as we have seen, reflecting differences in the industrial composition of employment from state to state. To what extent should each state be responsible for its own unemployment insurance costs (except to the limited extent that they can be passed on to consumers in other states in the form of higher prices), and to what extent should an attempt be made to spread the costs more evenly among the states through federal government contributions to state systems or federal assumption of some of the costs?

The rise in costs in recent years has been accompanied by serious deterioration of balances in some of the state funds, borrowing by a few states from the federal unemployment account under the provisions of the Reed Act of 1954, and very substantial increases in maximum tax rates in some of the states. By the middle of 1961, when the unemployment brought on by the 1960-61 recession had imposed a heavy drain on state funds, aggregate reserves, which had amounted to about 8 percent of taxable wages in the middle fifties, were down to $4.7 billion, or 4.8 percent of aggregate taxable wages. Moreover, the adequacy of

reserves varied greatly from state to state.[29] Although many of
the states had taken vigorous steps to raise their contributory
tax rates since 1958, others had displayed less concern over
maintaining the solvency of their funds (147).

In 1960, Congress amended the Reed Act to impose more
stringent penalties against states which lagged in the repayment
of advances from the federal unemployment account and which,
in the second and third full years after the advance, did not collect unemployment insurance taxes amounting to at least 2.7 percent of taxable wages in the state.[30] But should a state be eligible for federal assistance at all if it is in trouble partly because it has previously permitted its own average tax rate to
fall to an unduly low level? Recognition of this problem has led
to inclusion, in some of the recent proposals for reform of the
system, of a recommendation for a federal reinsurance fund which
would be used to reimburse the states for above-average unemployment insurance costs, but *only* if the state maintained a certain minimum average tax rate at all times.

The whole question of federal contributions to state systems is, of course, closely related to the question of whether the
federal government should require the states to maintain minimum
benefit standards, which was discussed above. Given the substantial variations in costs from state to state, some type of federal reinsurance or equalization program to aid the states in
meeting unusually high costs appears to be an important part of
any proposal for federal benefit standards, and has been included
in most recent proposals for reform of the system.

In addition, most of the proposals for permanent revision
call for an increase in the earnings base under the federal act
from $3,000 to some higher figure, though rarely by an amount

29If the highest costs experienced by each state in any 12-month
period in the previous 10 years are used as a standard against which to
measure the adequacy of reserves, 10 states had balances below this
amount, whereas, at the other extreme, 13 states had at least three
times this amount in their funds. See 163, p. 9.

30The penalties take the form of deductions from the tax-offset
credits available to employees under the federal unemployment tax (157).

which would restore the earnings base to its original relationship with earnings levels. It should be noted, in this connection, that the usual method of measuring unemployment insurance costs, in terms of the ratio of benefits to taxable wages, tends to overstate the extent to which costs have risen in recent years. Benefit costs amounted to only 1.8 percent of total covered wages in the fiscal year 1961, as compared with 2.9 percent of taxable wages.

Whether or not Congress decides to adopt permanent changes in the system, the provisions for federally financed restraining and readjustment allowances which have recently been adopted have significant implications for federal-state relationships, which will become even more important if such provisions are made permanent or continued over a long period of years. Although the Manpower Development and Training Act of 1962 provides that the states must bear 50 percent of the costs of retraining allowances or unemployment compensation paid to trainees after the middle of 1964, there may well be pressure for an amendment that would continue full federal financing of these payments after that date. Full federal financing of the adjustment benefits under the Trade Expansion Act may also represent a significant step toward greater federal involvement in the financing of unemployment compensation.

If the time has come for a thoroughgoing reexamination of the unemployment insurance program, as Lester suggests (177, p. 130), should serious consideration be given to the possibility of employee contributions? From time to time proposals have been made for an employee contribution but have received relatively little attention or study. An employee contribution amounting to 1 percent of payroll, or even less, would go far toward meeting the average costs of the program over a period of years and would give representatives of employee groups a considerably more effective voice in pressing for improvements in the system, as some labor spokesmen have recognized in recent years. It might also give them a more direct interest in preventing abuse.

The costs to workers resulting from an employee contributory tax (whose regressiveness would depend in part on where the earnings ceiling was set) should be weighed against both the short-run benefits which workers would derive from a more effective system and the longer-run contribution which improvements in the system would make to economic stability and economic growth. But precisely how should the proposal for an employee contribution be framed? Should the tax be imposed at the federal level and 1) used to finance grants-in-aid to the states to make their programs more effective, or 2) partially or wholly offset against employee contributions to their state funds? Or, alternatively, should a decision about employee contributions be left to the states? And would a uniform employee contribution call for a comparable minimum contribution from employers under state experience-rating systems? These are difficult questions, but the sharp increases in payroll tax liabilities of employers in recent years may arouse greater interest in them.

SUMMARY

The full implications of the steps we are taking to extend the duration of unemployment benefits and place greater emphasis on retraining programs are by no means apparent as yet. Not only will several years of experience be required before the effectiveness of these programs can be gauged, but it is far too early to hazard a guess as to how recently enacted or proposed federal legislation will affect federal-state financing relationships or to what extent they will lead to a reshaping of the existing federal-state unemployment insurance system.

Meanwhile, that program is not making as effective a contribution to restoring the wage losses of unemployed workers or maintaining economic stability as it might. Proposals to strengthen the system are hampered by continuing fears that higher benefit levels will enhance disincentives to work and by a financing system that tends to maximize the resistance of employers and state legislatures to tax increases. Although some of the proposals that have been made in recent years would certainly strengthen the system, not enough study has been given to such possibilities as cyclically graduated compensation, wider variations in maximum duration on the basis of employment records in a previous five- or ten-year period, the appropriate relationship between unemployment insurance and unemployment assistance, or a broader tax base in the form of employee or government contributions or some combination of the two. Moreover, we lack reliable data on such disputed issues as the costs of extending coverage to farm or domestic workers. Economists could make an exceedingly important contribution toward illuminating these questions.

6. CONCLUSIONS

The questions that have been discussed in connection with OASDI and unemployment compensation illustrate the more important economic issues that arise in welfare programs. These issues are also present, in only slightly different form, in other programs, including public assistance, which has been almost totally neglected by economists. Yet public assistance expenditures represent a substantial proportion of all welfare expenditures, and the importance of careful analysis of the relationship between public assistance policies and social insurance policies has been amply illustrated in our discussion of OASDI and unemployment compensation.

As Herman and Anne Somers (202) have emphasized, the American approach to the development of social security policy is pluralistic and is likely to remain so. Although this is undoubtedly true, the question as to whether we are creating a rather chaotic patchwork of uncoordinated and overlapping programs becomes increasingly critical as new legislation aimed at relieving the economic plight of the aged, the unemployed, and other groups appears on the statute books. A few economists, appalled at the piecemeal character of our approach to welfare policies, have espoused the so-called "negative tax" proposal. Under this scheme existing welfare programs would be abolished, and instead all family units with incomes above the amount necessary for a subsistence level of living would pay a progressive income tax, while every other family unit would receive a government subsidy (i.e., a negative tax) in an amount sufficient to bring its income up to the subsistence level. The "social dividend" scheme proposed by Lady Rhys-Williams in Great Britain is essentially similar (76, pp. 94-114). Although such a scheme would have the advantage of simplicity and perhaps of greater administrative efficiency, serious questions have been raised about its probable effects on incentives to work and to save, and it appears to have little political appeal in countries where the social insurance approach, with its emphasis on benefits as a matter of right, has become increasingly popular.

Even though the negative tax proposal seems impractical, it does serve to highlight the need for greater attention to the over-all impact of our complex array of welfare policies on the distribution of real income and on the stability and growth of the economy as a whole. Granted that particular welfare programs present issues deserving of a more careful study than they have recently received, probably the most important potential contribution of economists lies in this broader area.

Undoubtedly the most challenging questions have to do with the relationship between welfare policies and economic growth, both in developed and underdeveloped countries. Does a mature economy run a serious risk of retardation of growth if it fails to relieve pockets of poverty and places too little emphasis on investment in human resources, or is there a danger that undue concern with such problems will impede saving and capital formation? Does the need for increased saving in an immature economy preclude the possibility of emphasis on welfare policies in the early stages of development? Should underdeveloped countries pursue much the same path that industrialized countries have followed in the evolution of their welfare policies, or should they seek to devise welfare policies which are particularly designed to meet such problems as overly rapid population growth and malnutrition, as Titmuss and Abel-Smith (88) have urged in their admirable recent report prepared for the government of Mauritius? Given the growing emphasis on problems of economic growth and development, it seems highly likely that economists, even in the absence of exhortation, will devote increasing attention to these questions.

Appendix. THE FEDERAL OASDI SYSTEM AND THE FEDERAL-STATE UNEMPLOYMENT INSURANCE SYSTEM: DESCRIPTION OF PROVISIONS AT END OF 1961

OASDI

The Old-Age, Survivors, and Disability Insurance system is governed by the provisions of the Social Security Act of 1935, as amended. Originally the scheme provided only for monthly benefits to retired aged workers,[1] but in 1939 monthly benefits to survivors and to dependents of retired workers were added, and a small lump-sum death benefit was provided. The 1956 amendments inaugurated a limited program of disability insurance benefits, which has since been substantially expanded.[2]

Coverage. Coverage has also been greatly expanded during the last quarter of a century. The old-age insurance features of the original Social Security Act covered only employees working in industry and commerce, or about 60 percent of the labor force, but, beginning in 1950, a series of amendments extended the program until, today, approximately 90 percent of the labor force is

---

[1]It also provided for cash refunds to survivors or to workers reaching age 65 who had not been in covered employment long enough to qualify for monthly benefits. For an excellent summary of the legislative history of OASDI, see 120. For a useful bibliography on the American social security system, see 77. See also 84 and 85.

[2]The so-called "disability freeze," designed to maintain the insured status and to protect the average monthly wage of permanently and totally disabled workers, had been adopted under the 1954 amendments.

covered. About half of those who are excluded at any given time are self-employed persons and farm and domestic workers who do not meet certain minimum requirements as to the amount of their earnings or the length of time worked.[3] Other excluded workers are civilian employees of the federal government, who are covered by the civil service and other staff retirement systems; self-employed doctors; and police and firemen under state or local retirement systems in certain states. Coverage is available on an elective basis to most employees of state and local governments and nonprofit organizations, while ministers are eligible for coverage on an individual voluntary basis.

Eligibility. Benefits are payable to 1) retired workers, 2) to permanently and totally disabled workers, 3) to elderly wives or dependent husbands of retired or disabled workers, 4) to elderly widows, and to elderly widowers who have been dependent on a deceased worker, 5) to children of an eligible deceased, retired, or disabled worker who are under age 18 or have been permanently and totally disabled since before age 18, 6) to mothers of eligible children regardless of the mother's age, and 7) to dependent parents of deceased workers.

Originally, monthly old-age benefits were not payable until the age of 65, but in 1956 actuarially reduced benefits were made available for retired female workers and wives of retired workers at age 62, while full benefits were made payable to widows at age 62. Actuarially reduced benefits were made available for elderly men from age 62 to age 64 under the 1961 amendments (100).

In addition to the age and other eligibility conditions already mentioned, benefits may be received only if the primary beneficiary (the person whose earnings in covered employment have built up rights to benefits) has achieved insured status. Insured

[3] Although there are always some of these workers who cannot meet the requirements at any given time, the requirements are generally minimal, so that relatively few working people are excluded over their working lives (95). A farm laborer, for example, is credited with a quarter of coverage for each $100 of annual wages; an individual with creditable self-employment income of, in general, $400 or more is entitled to four quarters of coverage; and other individuals are credited with a quarter of coverage for each $50 or more of nonfarm wages in a calendar quarter.

status depends on quarters of coverage, and an individual may be "fully insured" or "currently insured." In general, fully insured status provides rights to retirement and survivorship benefits, whereas currently insured status provides them only for certain types of survivorship benefits. To qualify for disability benefits, a disabled worker must be fully insured and also have had at least 20 quarters of coverage in the 40 quarters before he became disabled. In addition, he must have been disabled six months.

To be fully insured, an individual must fulfill one of the following requirements: 1) have 40 quarters of coverage; or 2) have at least 6 quarters of coverage, including at least 1 quarter (acquired at any time after 1936) for every 4 quarters elapsing after 1950 (or age 21 if later) and before the year in which he reaches retirement age, dies, or becomes disabled. Currently insured status requires 6 quarters of coverage within the 13 quarters preceding death or entitlement to old-age benefits.

Finally, an individual claiming monthly benefits must satisfy the so-called retirement test—a feature of OASDI that has given rise to much controversy. The system was not intended to provide an annuity at a given age but was originally designed to provide monthly benefits only for elderly persons who were for all practical purposes completely retired. Cost considerations were important in the minds of those framing the Social Security Act—it would have been much more expensive to provide an annuity to every qualified individual who reached age 65—but, in addition, during the 1930s the view was widely held that elderly persons should be encouraged to retire in order to improve employment opportunities for younger workers. From 1950 on, under the influence of tighter labor market conditions and growing concern over the problem of employment opportunities for older persons, the retirement test was progressively liberalized (98 and 118). Since January, 1955, an individual claiming monthly benefits has been permitted to earn up to $1,200 a year without loss of benefits, but provisions affecting earnings in excess of $1,200 have been changed frequently. Under the 1961 amendments, one dollar in benefits is withheld for each two dollars of earnings between $1,200 and $1,700. Beyond that point one dollar of benefits is lost for every dollar of earnings (100). However, no benefit is withheld for any month in which the claimant neither earns wages of more than $100 nor renders substantial services in self-employment. This provision tends to give an advantage to persons whose earnings are irregularly distributed over the year.

It should be noted that under the retirement test benefits may be withheld, not only from retired workers whose earnings exceed the prescribed limits, but also from all other types of beneficiaries with earnings above the specified amounts.[4] The test does not, however, apply to individuals aged 72 or more. Such persons, it is argued, ought to have a chance before they die to receive some benefits on the basis of their years of contributions even if they go on working more or less indefinitely; and, since the number in this age group who earn more than the retirement test permits is very small, the costs are minimal.

Benefits. The monthly benefit payable to a retired or disabled worker is called the *primary insurance amount.* All other types of benefits—to dependents and survivors—are expressed as a percentage of this amount, which is based on the worker's average monthly wage in covered employment. In computing the average monthly wage, the starting date is usually December 31, 1950, or the last day of the year in which the individual reached age 21, whichever yields the higher amount. Certain periods of low or non-existent earnings may be eliminated ("dropped out") from the computation, as follows: 1) the five years of lowest earnings after 1950 and up to the year in which the person becomes eligible for benefits, dies, or becomes disabled; and 2) periods of total disability of at least six months' duration.

The benefit formula, which has been liberalized a number of times, is quite heavily weighted in favor of those with relatively low earnings. As most recently revised, in 1958, it calls for a primary benefit amounting to 58.85 percent of the first $110 of average monthly wage plus 21.4 percent of the next $290.[5] Earn-

---

[4]Under the 1960 amendments, however, a disability insurance beneficiary is allowed a period of 12 months of trial work during which his disability benefits or freeze will not be terminated solely because of such work.

ings in excess of $400 a month are not included in the computation of the average monthly wage, and, as we shall see, the maximum annual amount of earnings subject to contributory taxes is a corresponding sum, $4,800 a year. Also favoring those with low earnings is the provision for a minimum monthly benefit, which was raised from $33 to $40 a month under the 1961 amendments.

An eligible wife, dependent husband, or child of a retired or disabled worker receives half of the primary benefit amount, while an elderly widow, dependent widower, or a single surviving dependent parent receives 82½ percent of the primary benefit.[6] Each eligible child of a deceased worker is entitled to three-fourths of the primary benefit, as is the mother of such children, but the maximum family benefit is 80 percent of the primary benefit or $254, whichever is less. The lump-sum death benefit is three times the primary monthly benefit but not more than $255.

The benefit for a single retired worker may vary from $40 to $127 under the present schedule. In July, 1962, the average benefit received by a single retired worker was approximately $76 a month. The benefit for a disabled worker is computed in the same manner as the benefit for a retired worker. When he reaches the age of 65, his benefit is converted to a retirement benefit.

Retired workers and their dependents represent the largest group of beneficiaries, accounting for 10.3 of the 14.3 million persons receiving benefits from the program in an average month in 1960. Of the remaining beneficiaries, 3.4 million were receiving survivors' benefits, while 543 thousand were disabled workers or their dependents (83, p. 6).

Financing. OASDI is designed to be a self-supporting system, financed by taxes on the earnings of workers in covered employment. It was anticipated from the beginning that the cost of the program would gradually increase as the proportion of elderly

[5]However, this applies only to averages computed from the end of 1950. For averages computed from 1937 on, the 1939 formula (somewhat modified) is used in conjunction with a conversion table.

[6]Before the 1961 amendments became effective, widows, dependent widowers, and dependent parents received 75 percent of the primary amount.

people in the population and the percentage eligible for benefits rose. The 1935 act called for a schedule of contributions that would be increased from 1 percent of taxable wages on both employer and employee in 1937 to 3 percent in 1949. The rates were set in such a way that contributions would exceed benefits for some years. Thus a sizable reserve fund would be built up which, together with accrued interest, would be available to meet rising benefit payments in later years.

As a result of rising employment and wage levels, contributions during the 1940s were much higher than had been anticipated, and the tax rates were not raised in accordance with the original schedule. In 1950, when benefits were raised, the entire financing program was reviewed, and a new schedule of gradually increasing rates was established. These rates have been revised several times since 1950.

At present (1963), employer and employee each pay $3\frac{5}{8}$ percent on the first $4,800 of the employee's annual earnings. A self-employed person pays 5.4 percent on the first $4,800 of his net earnings. The rate applicable to employers and employees is scheduled to rise gradually to $4\frac{5}{8}$ percent in 1969, while that on the self-employed will rise to 6.9 percent (100, p. 7). It should be noted that the ceiling on annual taxable earnings was originally $3,000, but was gradually increased to $4,800 between 1950 and 1958.

THE FEDERAL-STATE UNEMPLOYMENT INSURANCE SYSTEM

Under the provisions of the Social Security Act of 1935, the federal government sought to induce the states to enact unemployment insurance laws through a tax-offset device, under which employers in all the states would be subject to a federal payroll tax of 3 percent but would be liable for only one-tenth of this tax if they were contributing to a state unemployment insurance system which embodied certain features set forth in the federal act.

The device proved to be extremely effective. Within two years after adoption of the Social Security Act, all the states had enacted unemployment insurance legislation (205 and 208).

The proceeds of the federal tax have been used for grants to the states to meet administrative costs and, in recent years, for advances to states with insufficient reserves. States are required to adopt administrative procedures designed to ensure prompt and full payment of benefits when due and to select and maintain their personnel on a merit basis. They must also 1) make benefit payments through a public employment office, 2) deposit their unemployment insurance funds in a special account maintained by the federal treasury, in order to ensure centralized management of the investment of the funds, 3) provide unemployed workers with the right of appeal to impartial tribunals in disputes over benefit claims, and 4) permit unemployed workers to refuse jobs which do not meet prescribed standards without having their benefits withheld. More specifically, the unemployed worker may refuse a job 1) that is vacant because of a strike or lockout, 2) in which wages, hours, or other conditions of employment are substantially less favorable than those prevailing for similar work in the area, or 3) in which he would be required to join a company union or refrain from membership in a bona fide labor organization as a condition of employment.

In addition, the federal law influences the state laws in certain other ways. Those types of employment that are exempt from the federal unemployment insurance tax—now embodied in the Federal Unemployment Tax Act—are also likely to be exempt from state coverage, although there are some exceptions, as we shall see. Experience-rating provisions of state laws are also affected by certain requirements of the federal act. However, the states are free to frame their own provisions on such vital features as amount and duration of benefits, eligibility provisions, and, to a large extent, their tax schedules.

Coverage. About three out of every five workers in the United States are covered by unemployment insurance. The Federal Unemployment Tax Act 1) does not apply to the self-employed (who tend to be excluded from unemployment insurance in all countries, for rather obvious reasons), 2) excludes agricultural workers, domestic servants, state and local government employees, and employees of nonprofit institutions, and 3) applies only to firms with four or more employees.[7] The state unemployment insurance laws cover all employment subject to the federal act and in some respects go beyond it. By the end of 1961, for example, 23 states and the District of Columbia were covering firms with fewer than four workers, and 20 of these jurisdictions covered firms with one or more employees.[8] Thirty states had some sort of elective or mandatory provisions for covering certain state and/or local government employees, and a few states had provisions covering other types of employment excluded from the federal act.[9] Federal civilian employees and ex-servicemen have been covered under special federal legislation which provides that benefits for these persons are financed through federal funds but are administered by the states and paid in accordance with the provisions of the state laws (154 and 206).

Eligibility. To be eligible for unemployment insurance a covered worker must have had sufficient earnings or employment in the base period (approximately the preceding year), must be unemployed through no fault of his own, and must be able to work and available for work.

The requirement that a jobless worker must have had sufficient earnings or employment in the preceding year is designed to ensure that benefits are paid only to persons with substantial recent participation in the labor force and on whose behalf a certain minimum amount of contributions has been paid into the system.[10] Most of the states require a minimum amount of earnings in the base period, but the amounts vary greatly, ranging, at the

[7]Originally the federal act applied to firms with eight or more employees. Useful articles on changes in state laws appear frequently in 218 and 221.

[8]However, only seven jurisdictions have broad coverage of one or more workers employed by the firm at any time during the year.

[9]Hawaii, for example, covered employees of large farms. Most of the states permit elective coverage by private employers of types of employment excluded under the compulsory features of the law, but relatively few workers have been brought in under these provisions.

[10]The laws generally define the base period as a period of a year (or four calendar quarters) ending several months before the date on which the claimant applies for benefits, to ensure that the necessary earnings records will be available.

end of 1961, from $150 in Hawaii to $800 in the state of Washington.[11] As wages have risen, there has been a tendency to raise base-period earnings requirements. In addition, as the states have gained experience with the program, there has been a tendency to add requirements calling for distribution of earnings over several quarters, in order to make it more difficult for seasonal and intermittent workers to qualify. California, for example, requires minimum earnings of $600, but if more than 75 percent of the claimant's base-period earnings were concentrated in a single quarter, he must have earned $750 or 30 times his weekly benefit amount, whichever is lower.

An alternative approach, which largely gets around the need for adjustment as earnings levels rise, is to require a minimum number of weeks of employment in the base period. Ten states have this type of provision, with the required number of weeks ranging from 14 in Michigan to 20 in New York and three other states.[12] However, New York and Wisconsin have recently adopted provisions which also take into account a record of substantial employment in the two years preceding the claim for benefits, if the claimant fails to meet the basic requirement by a few weeks.[13]

It requires only cursory inspection of the variations in these provisions to recognize that they will have substantially differing effects on the extent to which seasonal or intermittent workers can build up eligibility for benefits. Some of the states attempt

[11]It should be noted that some of the states express the minimum earnings requirement in terms of a multiple of the individual's weekly benefit amount, whereas others express it as a flat amount.

[12]It should be noted that the claimant must have earned at least a minimum amount in each of the required weeks of employment, e.g., $15 in New York, under many of these laws. Thus, the problem of erosion of the restrictiveness of the requirements as earnings levels rise is not altogether absent, but it is less critical than in the states that rely on an earnings requirement.

[13]In New York, a claimant who has had at least 15 weeks of employment (averaging at least $15 a week) in the preceding 52 weeks and 40 weeks in the preceding 104 weeks may qualify, while in Wisconsin he may qualify if he has had at least 14 but less than 18 weeks in the preceding 52 weeks and 55 or more weeks in the preceding 104 weeks.

to limit the payment of benefits to seasonal workers through additional provisions which classify certain industries as seasonal and restrict eligibility for benefits in off-season periods, but such provisions have posed serious administrative difficulties (177, p. 53 and 198).

Every claimant is required to register for work at a public employment office and, as already indicated, he must be able to work and be available for work.[14] In addition some state laws have special provisions restricting the eligibility of students or of married or pregnant women under certain conditions. Many of the states, moreover, have specific requirements designed to ensure that claimants actively seek work. Highly significant, also, in the last few years has been the adoption by a number of states of special provisions permitting the payment of benefits to workers enrolled in approved training and retraining programs, i.e., such workers are no longer to be declared ineligible because they are unavailable for work during a period of training.

Even though a claimant is able to work and available for work he may be disqualified for unemployment benefits if he has quit his job without good cause, been discharged for misconduct, refuses an offer of suitable work, or is directly involved in a labor dispute. In the case of a labor dispute, the disqualification generally lasts for the duration of the dispute. In the other situations, many of the states deny benefits only for a period of approximately six weeks or so, others for considerably longer periods, and some go so far as to deny benefits for the entire duration of the ensuing unemployment. In general, there has been a tendency to make the disqualification provisions more severe as time has gone on. However, many of the states continue to take the attitude that disqualification periods should not be unduly long, since, for example, a worker who voluntarily quit his job without good cause, but who has not succeeded in finding another job at the end of six weeks or so, must be considered in-

[14]The requirements that a claimant must be able to work and available for work have given rise to a host of problems of interpretation, which cannot be fully discussed. The classic study on these questions is 140. See, also, 169, pp. 39-44.

voluntarily unemployed. Although the disqualification provisions have been a focus of controversy and have given rise to many appeals cases, the number of claimants who are disqualified in any given year represents a very small fraction of all claimants.[15]

Benefit amounts. Weekly benefit amounts are related to a worker's previous earnings in covered employment in all the states. In general, the state laws originally aimed at paying weekly benefits that would amount to about 50 percent of the jobless worker's former weekly earnings. However, they also set maximum and minimum weekly benefit amounts, and, in the face of rising wages, the maximum amounts tended to become more restrictive unless they were frequently adjusted upward. In fact, most states have increased maximum benefits a number of times, but the adjustments have tended to lag behind wage increases. As a result, the maxima tend to be lower in relation to average wages than they were in the early years of the program.

Late in 1961, the maximum weekly benefit (excluding allowances for dependents) varied from $28 in Alabama to $55 in California, with 21 states providing maxima of $40 or more.[16] In eight states, under provisions adopted within recent years, the maximum amount is automatically adjusted to reflect changes in wage levels. Most of these states provide that the maximum amount must equal 50 percent of the average weekly wage in the state, but in a few cases it is set at 52½ or 55 percent. In the 12 jurisdictions providing dependents' benefits, the maximum weekly amount, including dependents' allowances, ranged at the end of 1961 from $30 in the District of Columbia to $70 in Alaska.[17]

One result of the erosion of maxima has been that well over half of new claimants have been eligible for maximum benefits in many of the states in recent years (139, Table B-5). Most of these claimants necessarily receive benefits that are considerably less than half their former earnings under the benefit formulas in effect in these states.

[15]In 1959, disqualifications for all reasons amounted to only about 2 percent of all claimant contacts.

[16]Puerto Rico, which has a maximum of only $16, is excluded from the above comparison.

[17]In Massachusetts, the maximum is the average weekly wage.

Since a worker's base-period earnings may have varied substantially from week to week, the problem of arriving at an appropriate measure of a claimant's normal weekly earnings in the base period has posed difficulties. Most of the states now use a formula under which the weekly benefit amount to which a claimant will be entitled is expressed as a fraction of his highest quarterly earnings in his base period. In nine states, the fraction is 1/26 of earnings in the highest quarter, i.e., is designed to restore 50 percent of a worker's average weekly earnings in a 13-week quarter. Other states use slightly larger fractions, while a few states have a variable formula under which low earners receive a somewhat larger fraction than high earners. Finally, there are approximately a dozen states in which benefit amounts are expressed as a percentage of annual earnings or of average weekly earnings in the base period.

Benefits are also paid to the partially unemployed, provided their earnings are less than the weekly benefit amount to which they would be entitled if fully unemployed. To provide an incentive for part-time work, the benefit for partial unemployment is usually somewhat higher than the difference between the weekly benefit amount and the individual's part-time earnings.

Benefit duration. The unemployment insurance system has been designed to tide a worker over a relatively short period of unemployment—not to provide benefits throughout a lengthy period of joblessness. (With certain qualifications, this is also true of unemployment insurance systems in other countries.) Most of the state laws explicitly establish a relationship between the individual claimant's earnings or employment record in the base period and the maximum number of weeks for which he may receive benefits, through a variable formula under which those who can barely meet the qualifying requirements will be eligible for fewer weeks of benefits than those with larger earnings or steadier employment in the base period. Eleven states and Puerto Rico, however, provide benefits for the same maximum period to all qualified claimants.

There has been a decided tendency to liberalize provisions affecting maximum duration, as compared with the early state laws, which typically provided for a maximum duration of 16 weeks in a given year. By the fall of 1961, nearly three-fourths of the states allowed benefits for a maximum period of 26 weeks (disregarding special provisions for extended benefits under certain circumstances), although many of these states used a variable formula under which some workers might qualify for as few as, say, 10 or 12 weeks. There were nine states with somewhat more liberal provisions, typically allowing a maximum of 30 weeks, while six states and Puerto Rico had maxima below 26 weeks.

In addition, seven states have adopted provisions in recent years under which the maximum duration of benefits is automatically extended (usually by 50 percent of normal duration) if unemployment in the state rises to a certain level, e.g., 6 percent of covered employment. Concern over the substantial proportion of claimants who were exhausting benefits also led the federal government to intervene in both the 1957-58 and 1960-61 recessions with legislation providing for temporary extension of benefits, for a maximum period of 50 percent of the maximum set in the state law. The 1961 law also provided that the extension was not to exceed 13 weeks in any of the states. The 1958 law, which provided for advances to states electing to participate, was implemented only in 16 states and the District of Columbia, whereas the 1961 law, which provided for financing the extended benefits through a temporary increase in the federal unemployment tax, became applicable in all the states.

It should be noted that most of the states require a waiting period, usually a week after the individual becomes unemployed, before payment of benefits can begin. Here, too, there has been substantial liberalization over the years, since most of the original laws imposed a two-week or longer waiting period.

Financing. Under the Federal Unemployment Tax Act, covered employers in all the states are subject to a federal unemployment tax of 3.1 percent of taxable earnings in their establishments. However, the effective federal tax is only 0.4 percent, since employers contributing to an approved state system receive a credit of not more than 2.7 percent against the federal tax. Moreover, this credit of 2.7 percent is allowed even if the tax an

employer actually pays to his state fund is below 2.7 percent,
under the provisions of an experience-rating system. The proceeds of the federal tax are used for grants to the states to cover
administrative expenses and, since 1954, have also been used
for advances to states whose unemployment insurance funds fell
below certain specified levels. In 1960, Congress raised the federal tax, which had previously been 3.0 percent (or, effectively,
0.3 percent) to provide more funds for these purposes.

Moreover, in 1963 and 1964, employers must pay a federal
tax of 3.5 percent (or an effective tax of 0.8 percent), with the
procceds of the temporary increase of 0.4 percent earmarked to
meet the costs of the extended benefits made available under the
Temporary Extended Unemployment Compensation Act of 1961.

The federal tax has applied, from the beginning, only to annual earnings up to $3,000 for any given employer, and although
there have been numerous proposals to increase the earnings
base to reflect the rise in wages that has occurred in the last
quarter of a century Congress has thus far not acted to do so.
The states, too, have been reluctant to raise their earnings
bases. At the end of 1961, all but nine states retained the earnings base of $3,000 which had been adopted under all the origi-
nal state laws. Of the remaining states, seven had increased the
base to $3,600, while California had raised it to $3,800 and
Alaska to $7,200. The controversy over whether increased revenue
should be obtained through increasing tax rates or raising the
earnings base has given rise to some interesting debates over
the distribution of the tax burden, which have been mentioned on
p. 111, above.

Influenced by the federal provisions, nearly all the states
rely exclusively on a payroll tax levied on covered employers to
finance their systems, although three (Alabama, Alaska, and
New Jersey) also require a small employee contribution. Furthermore, experience-rating systems are universal, outside of Alaska,
although in recent years several states have temporarily suspended them to meet the problem of rising costs.

Experience rating is a method which permits the tax rates of
individual employers to be adjusted on the basis of their experi-

ence with unemployment. The Wisconsin law of 1932 provided for a separate reserve account for each covered employer, out of which benefits would be paid to his employees who became unemployed. In most of the states, however, benefits are paid from pooled funds, although separate records are maintained for purposes of experience rating.

The Federal Unemployment Tax Act sets forth certain requirements for experience-rating systems, but within the framework of these requirements state systems vary greatly. There are five different types of experience-rating formulas in use. The reserve-ratio formula, which is by far the most popular, calls for variations in employer tax rates based on the ratio C–B/P, where C equals the employer's total contributions since the law went into effect, B equals the total benefits that have been paid to his employees, and P equals his average payroll during the previous three years (except for newly covered employers, for whom P in some states equals last year's payroll).

Many of the states have several alternative tax schedules. Which of these will be in effect in any given year will depend on the status of the reserve. If the reserve falls below a given point, in relation to taxable wages, a higher schedule will automatically come into effect in most states. In Wisconsin, however, tax reductions are likely to occur in a recession under a provision which calls for a reduced tax schedule to go into effect when total benefit payments rise above a certain point. Arizona has a tax policy which is designed to minimize fluctuations in the average tax rate from year to year (177, pp. 71-73).

A more adequate idea of a typical experience-rating system may be had by considering that of California, which is based on the reserve-ratio formula. In the middle 1950s, the basic schedule set forth in the California law was as follows:

Employer's reserve ratio (in percent)	Contribution rate (in percent)
0 - 7.5	2.7
7.5 - 9.0	2.5
9.0 - 10.0	2.0
10.0 - 11.0	1.5
11.0 - 100.0	1.0

However, the law also provided for a lower schedule which became effective whenever the balance in the state fund exceeded 7.1 percent of total taxable wages, and it was this lower schedule that was actually in effect. It provided for rates ranging from 0 to 2.7 percent, with gradations that were finer and more numerous than those in the basic schedule.[18] The law also provided that if the balance in the fund should ever fall to less than one and one-half times the total amount of benefits paid during the preceding calendar year experience rating would be temporarily suspended, and all covered employers would be subject to a tax of 2.7 percent.

In response to higher benefit costs and declining reserve funds in recent years, California, like a good many other states, has made a number of adjustments in its tax schedule. Currently (1962) the tax schedule in effect—the highest of several alternative schedules now set forth in the law—imposes rates ranging from 1.7 to 3.0 percent, while employers are also subject to a uniform 0.5 percent tax, imposed to assure the solvency of the state fund and not to be credited to individual employer accounts but only to the general fund. Thus employers are currently paying state tax rates ranging from 2.2 to 3.5 percent. Reportedly, employers were willing to support the imposition of the 0.5 percent tax in order to guarantee the long-run preservation of the experience-rating system. The law also provides for two lower schedules (adopted in 1959), with rates ranging from 0.3 to 3.0 percent, which would become effective if the balance in the fund rose to specified levels (183, December, 1960, September, 1961, and December, 1961).

California's experience in the last few years has been fairly typical. Whereas, before 1958, a state tax schedule which imposed a maximum rate above 2.7 percent was a rarity, rates above that level are now quite common. Late in 1961, it was reported that 26 states provided for maximum tax rates of 2.9 percent or more, and, in states like Michigan and Pennsylvania, which had been experiencing particularly high costs, the maximum rate in effect was considerably higher than this.

[18]In 1955, 13 percent of all covered employers in the state were benefitting from the 0 rate.

REFERENCES

ECONOMIC THEORY, ECONOMIC POLICY, AND INCOME STUDIES

1. Dorothy S. Brady. "Family Budgets: A Historical Survey," *Monthly Labor Review*, LVI (February, 1948), 171-75.
2. J. A. Brittain. "Some Neglected Features of Britain's Income Leveling," *Papers and Proceedings of the 72nd Annual Meeting of The American Economic Association, American Economic Review*, L (May, 1960), 593-603.
3. M. Bronfenbrenner, T. Yamane, and C. H. Lee. "A Study in Redistribution and Consumption," *Review of Economics and Statistics*, XXXVII (May, 1955), 149-59.
4. P. Cagan. "The Impact on Aggregate Saving," in Tested Knowledge of Business Cycles, pp. 63-64. New York, National Bureau of Economic Research, 1962. 42nd Annual Report.
5. A. M. Cartter. The Redistribution of Income in Postwar Britain. New Haven, Yale University Press, 1955.
6. J. M. Clark. "An Appraisal of the Workability of Compensatory Devices," *Papers and Proceedings of the 51st Annual Meeting of the American Economics Association, American Economic Review*, XXIX (March, 1939), 194-208.
7. M. O. Clement. "The Quantitative Impact of Automatic Stabilizers," *Review of Economics and Statistics*, XLII (February, 1960), 56-61.
8. A. H. Conrad. "The Multiplier Effects of Redistributive Public Budgets," *Review of Economics and Statistics*, XXXVII (May, 1955), 160-73.
9. — "Redistribution Through Government Budgets in the United States, 1950," in A. T. Peacock, ed., Income Redistribution and Social Policy. London, Jonathan Cape, 1954.
10. E. F. Denison. "Income Types and the Size Distribution: Rela-

tion to Functional Distribution and Factor Compensation," *Papers and Proceedings of the 66th Annual Meeting of the American Economic Association, American Economic Review,* XLIV (May, 1954), 254-69.

11. — The Sources of Economic Growth in the United States and the Alternatives Before Us. New York, Committee for Economic Development, 1962.

12. J. S. Duesenberry. Income, Saving, and the Theory of Consumer Behavior. Cambridge, Mass., Harvard University Press, 1949.

13. J. S. Duesenberry, O. Eckstein, and G. Fromm. "A Simulation of the United States Economy in a Recession," *Econometrica,* XXVIII (October, 1960), 740-809.

14. Ernst Engel. "Die Produktions- und Consumtions-verhältnisse des Königreichs Sachsen," *Zeitschrift des statistischen Bureaus des Königlich Sachsischen Ministeriums des Innern* (November, 1857). Reprinted in the *Bulletin de l'Institut International de Statistique* (1895).

15. M. J. Farrell. "The New Theories of the Consumption Function," *Economic Journal,* LXIX (December, 1959), 678-96.

16. Robert Ferber. "Research on Household Behavior," *American Economic Review,* LII (March, 1962), 19-63.

17. Milton Friedman, A Theory of the Consumption Function. Princeton, Princeton University Press, 1957.

18. J. K. Galbraith. The Affluent Society. Boston, Houghton Mifflin Company, 1958.

19. George Garvy. "Functional and Size Distribution of Income and Their Meaning," *Papers and Proceedings of the 66th Annual Meeting of the American Economic Association, American Economic Review,* XLIV (May, 1954), 236-53.

20. Raymond Goldsmith. A Study of Saving in the United States. Princeton, Princeton University Press, 1955.

21. Selma F. Goldsmith. "The Relation of Census Income Distribution Statistics to Other Income Data," in Studies in Income and Wealth. Princeton, Princeton University Press, 1958. Vol. 23, pp. 65-107.

22. R. A. Gordon. Business Fluctuations. 2d ed. New York, Harper and Brothers, 1961.

23. A. H. Hansen. Economic Issues of the 1960's. New York, McGraw-Hill Book Company, Inc., 1960.

24. — Prepared statement, in Federal Tax Policy for Economic Growth and Stability, pp. 14-21. Washington, D. C., Government Printing Office, 1955. Papers submitted by panelists, November 9, 1955, U. S. Congress, Joint Committee on the Economic Report.

25. J. M. Jackson, "Wages, Social Income, and the Family," *Man-*

chester School of Economic and Social Studies, XXIX (January, 1961), 95-106.

26. H. G. Johnson. "The Macro-Economics of Income Redistribution," in A. T. Peacock, ed., Income Redistribution and Social Policy. London, Jonathan Cape, 1954.

27. J. M. Keynes. The General Theory of Employment, Interest, and Money. New York, Harcourt Brace and World, Inc., 1936.

28. Simon Kuznets. Capital in the American Economy: Its Formation and Financing. Princeton, Princeton University Press, 1961.

29. — National Income: A Summary of Findings. New York, National Bureau of Economic Research, 1946.

30. Helen H. Lamale. "Changes in Concepts of Income Adequacy Over the Last Century," *Papers and Proceedings of the 70th Annual Meeting of the American Economic Association, American Economic Review,* XLVIII (May, 1958), 291-99.

31. R. J. Lampman. "The Effectiveness of Some Institutions in Changing the Distribution of Income," *Papers and Proceedings of the 69th Annual Meeting of the American Economic Association, American Economic Review,* XLVII (May, 1957), 519-28.

32. J. B. Lansing and H. Lydall. "An Anglo-American Comparison of Personal Saving," *Bulletin of the Oxford University Institute of Statistics,* XXII (August, 1960), 225-58.

33. K. Lemberg, N. Ussing, and F. Zeuthen. "Redistribution of Income in Denmark," in A. T. Peacock, ed., Income Redistribution and Social Policy. London, Jonathan Cape, 1954.

34. Harold Lubell. "Effects of Income Redistribution on Consumers' Expenditures," *American Economic Review,* XXXIII (March, 1947), 157-70.

35. Julius Margolis. "A Comment on the Pure Theory of Public Expenditures," *Review of Economics and Statistics,* XXXII (November, 1955), 347-49.

36. J. T. Miner. Life Insurance Ownership Among American Families. Ann Arbor, Institute for Social Research, University of Michigan, 1947.

37. Franco Modigliani and Richard Brumberg. "Utility Analysis and the Consumption Function: An interpretation of Cross-Section Data," in K. K. Kurihara, ed., Post Keynesian Economics. New Brunswick, N. J., Rutgers University Press, 1954.

38. J. N. Morgan, M. H. David, W. J. Cohen, and H. E. Brazer. Income and Welfare in the United States. New York, McGraw-Hill Book Company, Inc., 1962.

39. R. A. Musgrave. "The Incidence of Tax Structure and Its Effects on Consumption," in Federal Tax Policy for Economic Growth and Stability, pp. 96-113. Washington, D. C., Government Printing Of-

fice, 1955. Papers submitted by panelists, November 9, 1955. U. S. Congress, Joint Committee on the Economic Report.

40. — The Theory of Public Finance. New York, McGraw-Hill Book Company, Inc., 1959.

41. R. A. Musgrave and Mary S. Painter. "The Impact of Alternative Tax Structures on Personal Income and Savings," *Quarterly Journal of Economics*, LXII (August, 1948), 475-99.

42. K. E. Poole. Public Finance and Economic Welfare. New York, Rinehart and Company, Inc., 1956.

43. Earl R. Rolph. The Theory of Fiscal Economics. Berkeley and Los Angeles, University of California Press, 1954.

44. G. Rottier and J. F. Albert. "The Social Services and Income Redistribution in France," in A. T. Peacock, ed., Income Redistribution and Social Policy. London, Jonathan Cape, 1954.

45. P. A. Samuelson. "Principles and Rules in Modern Fiscal Policy: A Neo-Classical Reformulation," in Money, Trade, and Economic Growth, pp. 157-76. New York, The Macmillan Company, 1951.

46. — "Diagrammatic Exposition of a Theory of Public Expenditures," *Review of Economics and Statistics*, XXXVII (November, 1955), 350-56.

47. — "The Pure Theory of Public Expenditures," *Review of Economics and Statistics*, XXXVI (November, 1954), 387-89.

48. A. M. Smithies. "Federal Budgeting and Fiscal Policy," in H. S. Ellis, ed., A Survey of Contemporary Economics. Philadelphia and Toronto, Blakiston Company, 1949.

49. Eleanor M. Snyder, "Cost of Living Indexes for Special Classes of Consumers," in Government Price Statistics, pp. 337-72. Washington, D. C., Government Printing Office, 1961. Hearings Before the Subcommittee on Economic Statistics, Joint Economic Committee, U. S. Congress, 87th Cong., 1st sess., Part I, January 24, 1961.

50. R. M. Solow. "Income Inequality Since the War," in R. E. Freeman, ed., Postwar Economic Trends in the United States. New York, Harper and Brothers, 1960.

51. 1960 Survey of Consumer Finances. Ann Arbor, Survey Research Center, University of Michigan, 1961.

52. R. M. Titmuss. Income Distribution and Social Change. London, Allen and Unwin, 1962.

SOCIAL SECURITY AND SOCIAL WELFARE, GENERAL

53. Brian Abel-Smith. "Social Security," in Morris Ginsberg, ed., Law and Opinion in England in the 20th Century. London, Stevens, 1959.

54. J. D. Brown. "The American Philosophy of Social Insurance," *Social Service Review,* XXX (March, 1956), 1-8.

55. Eveline M. Burns. "Issues in Social Security Financing," in Social Security in the United States. Berkeley, Institute of Industrial Relations, University of California, 1961. Four lectures presented by the Chancellor's Committee on the 25th Anniversary of the Social Security Act, April-May, 1961.

56. — Social Security and Public Policy. New York, Toronto, and London, McGraw-Hill Book Company, Inc., 1956.

57. — Toward Social Security. New York and London, McGraw-Hill Book Company, Inc., 1936.

58. Earl F. Cheit and Margaret S. Gordon, eds. Occupational Disability and Public Policy. To be published.

59. The Cost of Social Security, 1949-1957. Geneva, International Labour Office, 1961.

60. P. H. Douglas. Social Security in the United States. New York and London, McGraw-Hill Book Company, Inc., 1936.

61. Paul Durand. La Politique Contemporaine de Sécurite Sociale. Paris, Librarie Dalloz, 1953.

62. W. A. Friedlander. Introduction to Social Welfare. 2d ed. Englewood Cliffs, N. J., Prentice-Hall, Inc., 1957.

63. Henning Friis. "Comparison of Benefits in Danish Social Security Legislation," *Bulletin of the International Social Security Association,* XII (January-February, 1959), 15-18.

64. C. W. Gilmore. "Trust Funds and National Output," *Southern Economic Journal,* XXIV (July, 1957), 41-53.

65. S. E. Harris. The Economics of Social Security. New York and London, McGraw-Hill Book Company, Inc., 1941.

66. Thomas Karter. "Voluntary Agency Expenditures for Health and Welfare from Philanthropic Contributions," *Social Security Bulletin,* XXI (February, 1958), 14-18.

67. Pierre Laroque. "Major Issues Raised by Contemporary Trends in Income Security Policies," in J. E. Russell, ed., National Policies for Education, Health, and Social Services. New York, Russell and Russell. Inc., 1961.

68. R. A. Lester. "The Nature and Level of Income Security for a Free Society," in J. E. Russell, ed., National Policies for Education, Health, and Social Services, Garden City, N. Y., Doubleday and Company, Inc., 1955.

69. Elizabeth Liefmann-Keil. "Index-based Adjustments for Social Security Benefits," *International Labour Review,* LXXIX (May, 1959), 487-510.

70. Ida C. Merriam. Social Security Financing. Washington, D. C., U. S. Social Security Administration, 1952. Bureau Report No. 17.

71. — "Social Security Programs and Economic Stability," in Policies to Combat Depression. Princeton, Princeton University Press, 1956. A conference of the Universities-National Bureau Committee for Economic Research.

72. — "Social Welfare Expenditures, 1960-61," *Social Security Bulletin*, XXV (November, 1962), 3-13.

73. — "Social Welfare Programs in the United States," *Social Security Bulletin*, XVI (February, 1953), 3-12.

74. Selma J. Mushkin and Anne de Scitovsky. "A Formula for Social Insurance Financing," *American Economic Review*, XXXV (September, 1945), 646-52.

75. Selma J. Mushkin, Anne de Scitovsky, and Leila N. Small. Social Insurance Financing in Relation to Consumer Income and Expenditures. Washington, D. C., Government Printing Office, 1946. Bureau Memorandum No. 63, U. S. Social Security Board.

76. A. T. Peacock. The Economics of National Insurance. London, Hodge, 1952.

77. "References on the Origin and Development of Social Security in the United States," *Social Security Bulletin*, Anniversary Issue, XXIII (August, 1960), 71-74.

78. Report to the President of the Committee on Economic Security. Washington, D. C., Government Printing Office, 1935.

79. J. J. Ribas. "Observations on the Financing of Social Security in the Common Market Countries," *International Labour Review*, LXXXIV (July-August, 1961), 26-49.

80. J. H. Richardson. Economic and Financial Aspects of Social Security. London, Allen and Unwin, 1960.

81. Karl de Schweinitz. England's Road to Social Security. Philadelphia, University of Pennsylvania Press, 1943.

82. Social Insurance and Allied Services. Report by Sir William Beveridge. London, H. M. Stationery Office, and New York, The Macmillan Company, 1942.

83. *Social Security Bulletin: Annual Statistical Supplement*, 1960.

84. "Social Security in the United States," *Bulletin of the International Social Security Association*, XIV (October, 1961), 541-609.

85. "Social Security in the United States of America," *Bulletin of the International Social Security Association*, X (March-April, 1957), 87-102.

86. Social Security Programs Throughout the World, 1961. Washington, D. C., Government Printing Office, 1961. U. S. Social Security Administration.

87. R. M. Titmuss. Essays on the Welfare State. New Haven, Yale University Press, 1959.

88. R. M. Titmuss and Brian Abel-Smith. Social Policies and Popula-

tion Growth in Mauritius. London, Methuen and Company, Ltd., 1961.

89. Übersicht Über die Soziale Sicherung in der Bundesrepublik Deutschland, Stand: 1. April 1960. Bonn, Bundesministerium für Arbeit und Sozialordnung, 1960.

90. E. E. Witte. Development of the Social Security Act. Madison, University of Wisconsin Press, 1962.

OASDI AND THE ECONOMICS OF AGING

91. Brian Abel-Smith, "State Pensions and the Age of Retirement," in Wilma Donahue, Clark Tibbitts, and R. H. Williams, eds., Psychological and Social Processes of Aging: An International Research Seminar. To be published.

92. Background Paper on Income Maintenance. Prepared for the White House Conference on Aging, January 9-12, 1961. Washington, D. C., 1960.

93. "Budget for an Elderly Couple: Estimated Cost, October, 1950," *Monthly Labor Review,* LXXIII (September, 1951), 304-6.

94. J. J. Carroll. Alternative Methods of Financing Old-Age, Survivors, and Disability Insurance. Ann Arbor, Institute of Public Administration, University of Michigan, 1960.

95. Victor Christgau. "Old-Age, Survivors, and Disability Insurance After Twenty-Five Years," *Social Security Bulletin,* XXIII (August, 1960), 20-30.

96. Ewan Clague. Statement, in Retirement Income of the Aging, pp. 87-122. Washington, D.C., Government Printing Office, 1961. Hearings before the Subcommittee on Retirement Income of the Special Committee on Aging, U. S. Senate, 87th Cong., 1st sess, Part I, July 12-13, 1961.

97. R. M. Clark. Economic Security for the Aged in the United States and Canada: A Report Prepared for the Government of Canada. Ottawa, Queen's Printer, 1960.

98. W. J. Cohen. Retirement Policies Under Social Security. Berkeley and Los Angeles, University of California Press, 1957.

99. – Statement, in The Aged and the Aging in the United States, pp. 3-32. Washington, D. C., Government Printing Office, 1959. Hearings before the Subcommittee on Problems of the Aged and Aging, Committee on Labor and Public Welfare, U. S. Senate, 86th Cong., 1st sess., Part I, June 16-18, 1959.

100. W. J. Cohen and W. L. Mitchell. "Social Security Amendments of 1961: Summary and Legislative History," *Social Security Bulletin,* XXIV (September, 1961), 3-11.

101. Dorothy Cole, with J. E. G. Utting. The Economic Circumstances of Old People. Welwyn, Hertfordshire, England, The Codicote Press, 1962.

102. Nelson Cruikshank. Statement, in Problems of the Aged and Aging, pp. 182-95. Washington, D. C., Government Printing Office, 1959. Hearings before the Subcommittee on Problems of the Aged and Aging, Committee on Labor and Public Welfare, U. S. Senate, 86th Cong., 1st sess., Part I, June 16-18, 1959.

103. Economic Assumptions Underlying the Medium-Range Projections of the Federal Old-Age and Survivors Insurance and Disability Insurance Trust Funds, 1966-1975. Washington, D. C., U. S. Social Security Administration, 1961.

104. Employment and Retirement of Older Workers. Sacramento, State Printing Office, 1960. Report of the California Governor's Commission on the Employment and Retirement Problems of Older Workers.

105. Lenore A. Epstein. "Money Income of Aged Persons: A 10-Year Review, 1948 to 1958," Social Security Bulletin, XXII (June, 1959), 3-11.

106. — "The Aged in the Population and Their Income Sources," Social Security Bulletin, XXIV (July, 1961), 3-10.

107. Sidney Goldstein, Study of Consumer Expenditures, Incomes, and Savings: Consumption Patterns of the Aged. Philadelphia, University of Pennsylvania, 1960.

108. Margaret S. Gordon. "The Income and Assets of the Elderly and Their Implications for the Housing Market," in G. W. Grier, ed., Housing the Aging: Research Needs. Washington, D. C., Brookings Institution, 1962.

109. — "Income Security Programs and the Propensity to Retire," in Wilma Donahue, Clark Tibbitts, and R. H. Williams, eds., Psychological and Social Processes of Aging: An International Research Seminar. To be published.

110. — "Projecting Employment Opportunities for Middle-Aged and Older Workers," in Aging and the Economy. Papers presented at the 15th Annual University of Michigan Conference on Aging, June 18-20, 1962.

111. — "Work and Patterns of Retirement," in R. W. Kleemeier, ed., Aging and Leisure. New York, Oxford University Press, 1961.

112. R. A. Hohaus. "Equity, Adequacy, and Related Factors in Old Age Security," The Record, XXVII, Part I (June, 1938), 76-119.

113. Kurt Jantz. "Pension Reform in the Federal Republic of Germany," International Labour Review, LXXXIII (February, 1961), 136-55.

114. C. C. Killingsworth and Gertrude Schroeder. "Long-Range Cost

Estimates for Old-Age Insurance," *Quarterly Journal of Economics*, LXV (May, 1951), 199-213.

115. M. S. March. "President's Commission on Veterans' Pensions: Recommendations," *Social Security Bulletin*, XIX (August, 1956), 12-18, 32.

116. J. N. Morgan and Martin David. Prepared statement, in Retirement Income of the Aging, pp. 188–99. Washington, D. C., Government Printing Office, 1961. Hearings before the Subcommittee on Retirement Income, Special Committee on Aging, U. S. Senate, 87th Cong., 1st sess., Part I, July 12-13, 1961.

117. H. H. Mugge. "Concurrent Receipt of Public Assistance and Old-Age, Survivors, and Disability Insurance," *Social Security Bulletin*, XXIII (December, 1960), 12-25.

118. R. J. Myers. "Basis and Background of the Retirement Test Under the OASDI System," in Retirement Income of the Aging, pp. 18–27. Washington, D. C.: Government Printing Office, 1961. Hearings before the Subcommittee on Retirement Income of the Special Committee on Aging, U. S. Senate, 87th Cong., 1st sess., Part I, July 12-13, 1961.

119. — "Old-Age, Survivors, and Disability Insurance: Financing Basis and Policy Under the 1961 Amendments," *Social Security Bulletin*, XXIV (September, 1961), 12-19.

120. — "Old-Age, Survivors, and Disability Insurance Provisions: Summary of Legislation, 1935-58," *Social Security Bulletin*, XXII (January, 1959), 15-20.

121. National Superannuation: Labour's Policy for Security in Old Age. London, The Labour Party, 1957.

122. "New Graduated Retirement Benefits in Great Britain," *Social Security Bulletin*, XXII (September, 1959), 4-9.

123. Mollie Orshansky. "Budget for an Elderly Couple: Interim Revision by the Bureau of Labor Statistics," *Social Security Bulletin*, XXIII (December, 1960), 26-36.

124. The Purchasing Power of Social Security Benefits and Payments, 1940-1960. Division of Program Research, U. S. Social Security Administration, Washington, D. C., 1961. Research and Statistics Note No. 10.

125. Reasons for Retiring or Continuing at Work. London, H. M. Stationery Office, 1954. Great Britain, Ministry of Pensions and National Insurance.

126. S. H. Slichter. "Can the Economy Afford the Loss of Production of Its Older Workers or the Financial Burden of Maintaining Them? What is the Effect of Changes of the Business Cycle on Employment and Retirement Practices?" in Three Monographs on Subjects Related to Retirement of Older Workers, pp. 77-113. New

York, National Conference on Retirement of Older Workers, 1952.

127. W. F. Smith. Housing for the Elderly in California. Berkeley, Real Estate Research Program, Institute of Business and Economic Research, University of California, 1961.

128. Margaret L. Stecker. "Why Do Beneficiaries Retire? Who Among Them Return to Work?" *Social Security Bulletin,* XVIII (May, 1955), 3-12.

129. P. O. Steiner and Robert Dorfman. The Economic Status of the Aged. Berkeley and Los Angeles, University of California Press, 1957.

130. Margaret S. Stotz. "The BLS Interim Budget for a Retired Couple," *Monthly Labor Review,* LXXXIII (November, 1960), 1141-57.

131. H. E. Striner. "National Income, Wealth, and the Capacity of the Economy to Support Older People," in Aging and the Economy. To be published. Papers presented at the 15th Annual University of Michigan Conference on Aging, June 18-20, 1962.

132. W. E. Thompson. The Impact of Retirement. Unpublished doctoral dissertation, Cornell University, 1956.

133. W. E. Thompson and G. F. Streib. "Situational Determinants: Health and Economic Deprivation in Retirement," *Journal of Social Issues,* XIV, No. 2 (1958), 18-34.

134. Léon Troclet. "Joint-Holding of a Retirement Pension and Gainful Employment," in Clark Tibbitts and Wilma Donahue, eds., Social and Psychological Aspects of Aging. New York and London, Columbia University Press, 1962.

135. Unusual Patterns of OASDI Contributions in 1957-1959. U. S. Social Security Administration, Washington, D. C., 1960. Research and Statistics Note No. 9.

136. "Veterans' Pension Act of 1959," *Social Security Bulletin,* XXII (December, 1959), 18-21.

137. A. T. Welford. Ageing and Human Skill. London, Oxford University Press, 1958.

UNEMPLOYMENT INSURANCE, THE LABOR MARKET, AND RELATED SUBJECTS

138. L. P. Adams and R. A. Aronson. Workers and Industrial Change. Ithaca, Cornell University Press, 1957.

139. Adequacy of Benefits Under Unemployment Insurance. Washington, D. C., Government Printing Office, 1959. U. S. Bureau of Employment Security, BES No. U-70(B).

140. Ralph Altman. Availability for Work. Cambridge, Mass., Harvard University Press, 1950.

141. E. W. Bakke and others. Labor Mobility and Economic Opportunity.

Cambridge, Mass., Technology Press, Massachusetts Institute of Technology, and New York, John Wiley and Sons, Inc., 1954.

142. Gertrude Bancroft. The American Labor Force. New York, John Wiley and Sons, Inc., 1958.

143. — "Trends in the Labor Force," in William Haber and others, eds., Manpower in the United States: Problems and Policies, pp. 132-42. New York, Harper and Brothers, 1954.

144. J. M. Becker, S.J. The Adequacy of the Benefit Amount in Unemployment Insurance. Kalamazoo, The W. E. Upjohn Institute for Employment Research, 1961.

145. — The Problem of Abuse in Unemployment Benefits. New York, Columbia University Press, 1953.

146. Irving Bernstein. The Lean Years. Boston, Houghton Mifflin Company, 1960.

147. S. J. Blaustein. "The Challenge Facing the Unemployment Insurance System," Monthly Labor Review, LXXXIV (March, 1961), 242-49.

148. W. G. Bowen. The Wage-Price Issue: A Theoretical Analysis, pp. 284-93. Princeton, Princeton University Press, 1959.

149. Eveline M. Burns. British Unemployment Programs, 1920-1938. Washington, D. C., Social Science Research Council, 1941.

150. — Submitted statement, in Economic Security Act, pp. 1006-14. Washington, D. C., Government Printing Office, 1935. Hearings before the Committee on Finance, U. S. Senate, 74th Cong., 1st sess., January 22 to February 20, 1935, revised.

151. Characteristics of General Assistance in the United States. Washington, D. C., Government Printing Office, 1959. Report prepared by the U. S. Bureau of Public Assistance for the Special Committee on Unemployment Problems, U. S. Senate, 86th Cong., 1st sess.

152. Miriam I. Civic. "Jobless Pay Offsets to Wage Declines," The Conference Board Business Record, XV (March, 1958), 96-97, 115.

153. W. J. Cohen, William Haber, and Eva Mueller. The Impact of Unemployment in the 1958 Recession. Ann Arbor, Institute of Labor and Industrial Relations, University of Michigan and Wayne State University, 1960.

154. Comparison of State Unemployment Insurance Laws as of January 1, 1962. Washington, D. C., Government Printing Office, 1962. U. S. Bureau of Employment Security, BES No. U-141.

155. "Costs of Non-Statutory Social Security Schemes," International Labour Review, LXXVIII (October, 1958), 388-403.

156. Daily Labor Report, No. 113, June 13, 1961, pp. A-1 to A-3.

157. Daily Labor Report, No. 178, September 13, 1960, pp. A-2 to A-3.

158. Daily Labor Report, No. 199, November 12, 1959, pp. A-5 to A-7.

159. Daily Labor Report, No. 218, November 11, 1961, pp. F-1 to F-10.

160. W. S. Devino. Exhaustion of Unemployment Benefits During a Recession: A Case Study. East Lansing, Labor and Industrial Relations Center, Michigan State University, 1960.
161. P. H. Douglas. Statement, in Economic Security Act, pp. 892-96. Washington, D. C., Government Printing Office, 1935. Hearings before the Committee on Finance, U. S. Senate, 74th Cong., 1st sess., January 22 to February 20, 1935, revised.
162. Experience of Claimants Exhausting Benefit Rights Under Unemployment Insurance, 17 Selected States. Washington, D. C., Government Printing Office, 1958. U. S. Bureau of Employment Security, BES No. U-178.
163. "Financial Developments Under State UI Programs," *The Labor Market and Employment Security* (December, 1961), 6-9.
164. R. R. France. "Wages, Unemployment, and Prices in the United States, 1890-1932, 1947-1957," *Industrial and Labor Relations Review*, XV (January, 1962), 171-90.
165. Fringe Benefits, 1959. Chamber of Commerce of the United States, Economic Research Department, Washington, D. C., 1960.
166. Fringe Benefits, 1961. Chamber of Commerce of the United States, Economic Research Department, Washington, D. C., 1962.
167. V. R. Fuchs. "Action Programs to Deal with Unemployment," *Monthly Labor Review*, LXXXV (February, 1962), 131-32.
168. L. V. Fuller. The Supply of Agricultural Labor as a Factor in the Evolution of Farm Organization in California, pp. 19777-898. Washington, D. C., Government Printing Office, 1940. Exhibit 8762, Hearings, U. S. Senate Committee on Education and Labor, 76th Cong., 3rd sess., Part 54.
169. Margaret S. Gordon and R. W. Amerson. Unemployment Insurance. Berkeley, Institute of Industrial Relations, University of California, 1957.
170. H. M. Groves and Elizabeth Brandeis. "Economic Bases of the Wisconsin Unemployment Reserves Act," *American Economic Review*, XXIV (March, 1934), 38-52.
171. William Haber. "The U. S. Employment Service in a Changing Economy," in Studies in Unemployment, pp. 283-309. Washington, D. C., Government Printing Office, 1960. Prepared for the Special Committee on Unemployment Problems, U. S. Senate, 86th Cong., 2d sess.
172. A. H. Hansen. Statement, in Economic Security Act, pp. 447-58. Washington, D. C., Government Printing Office, 1935. Hearings Before the Committee on Finance, U. S. Senate, 74th Cong., 1st sess., January 22 to February 20, 1935, revised.
173. R. L. Hibbard. Discussion on a paper by H. M. Somers, in Proceedings of the Twelfth Annual Meeting of Industrial Relations Research Association, 1959, pp. 104-7.

174. Industry Cost Rates. Research and Statistics Report 352A, No. 10, California Department of Employment, May 14, 1958.

175. Labour Costs in European Industry. Geneva, International Labour Office, 1959.

176. R. A. Lester. "The Economic Significance of Unemployment Compensation," *Review of Economics and Statistics,* XLII (November, 1960), 349-72.

177. — The Economics of Unemployment Compensation. Princeton, Industrial Relations Section, Princeton University, 1962.

178. R. A. Lester and J. D. Brown. Statement, in Unemployment Compensation, pp. 267-68. Washington, D. C., Government Printing Office, 1959. Hearings before the Committee on Ways and Means, House of Representatives, 86th Cong., 1st sess., April 7, 8, 9, 10, 13, 14, 15, and 16, 1959.

179. R. A. Lester and C. V. Kidd. The Case Against Experience Rating in Unemployment Compensation. New York, Industrial Relations Counselors, Inc., 1939.

180. R. G. Lipsey. "The Relation Between Unemployment and the Rate of Change of Money Wage Rates in the United Kingdom, 1862-1957: A Further Analysis," *Economica,* XXVII, New Series (February, 1960), 1-31.

181. C. D. Long. The Labor Force Under Changing Income and Employment. Princeton, Princeton University Press, 1958.

182. C. A. Myers. "Experience Rating in Unemployment Compensation," *American Economic Review,* XXXV (June, 1945), 337-54.

183. *Newsletter,* California Department of Employment.

184. Occupational Pension Schemes. London, H. M. Stationery Office, 1958. Great Britain, Government Actuary.

185. Gladys L. Palmer. Labor Mobility in Six Cities. New York, Social Science Research Council, 1954.

186. H. S. Parnes. Research on Labor Mobility. New York, Social Science Research Council, 1954.

187. A. W. Phillips. "The Relation Between Unemployment and the Rate of Change of Money Wage Rates in the United Kingdom, 1861-1957," *Economica,* XXV, New Series (November, 1958), 283-99.

188. Population and Labor Force Projections for the United States, 1960 to 1975. Washington, D. C., Government Printing Office, 1959. U. S. Bureau of Labor Statistics, Bulletin No. 1242.

189. Progress Report, Automation Committee. Armour and Company and United Packinghouse Food and Allied Workers, AFL-CIO, and Amalgamated Meat Cutters and Butcher Workmen of North America, AFL-CIO, Chicago, 1961.

190. La protection des travailleurs en cas de perte de l'emploi. Euro-

pean Coal and Steel Community, High Authority, Luxembourg,
1961.

191. "Provisions of the Manpower Development and Training Act,"
Monthly Labor Review, LXXXV (May, 1962), 532-34.

192. Public Assistance: Report of the Advisory Council on Public Assistance Containing Findings and Recommendations. Washington,
D. C., Government Printing Office, 1960. U. S. Senate, 86th Cong.,
2d sess., Doc. No. 93.

193. Public Law 87-27. 87th Cong., 1st sess., May 1, 1961.

194. Report of the Committee on Education and Labor on the Manpower
Development and Training Act of 1961. Washington, D. C., Government Printing Office, 1961. U. S. House of Representatives,
87th Cong., 1st sess., Report No. 879.

195. G. F. Rohrlich. "Measuring the Impact of UI Benefit Payments in
a Recession," *The Labor Market and Employment Security* (July,
1958), 5-10.

196. A. M. Ross. "Do We Have a New Industrial Feudalism?" *American
Economic Review*, XLVIII (December, 1958), 903-20.

197. C. L. Schultze. Recent Inflation in the United States. Washington,
D. C., Government Printing Office, 1959. Study Paper No. 1, Materials Prepared in Connection With the *Study of Employment,
Growth and Price Levels*, Joint Economic Committee, U. S. Congress, 86th Cong., 1st sess.

198. "Seasonal Provisions in State Unemployment Insurance Laws,"
The Labor Market and Employment Security (July, 1957), 1-6, 49.

199. Senate Bill 2084 (1961). Introduced by Senator McCarthy and
others.

200. A. M. Skolnik. "Employee Benefit Plans, 1954-60," *Social Security Bulletin*, XXV (April, 1962), 5-16.

201. "Social Aspects of European Economic Co-operation," *International Labour Review*, LXXIV (August, 1956), 99-123.

202. H. M. and Anne R. Somers. "Unemployment Insurance and Workmen's Compensation," in Proceedings of the Ninth Annual Meeting of Industrial Relations Research Association, 1956, pp. 120-
44.

203. "The Trade Expansion Act of 1962," *Labor Market and Employment Security* (October, 1962), 1-3.

204. Unemployment Insurance and the Family Finances of the Unemployed. Washington, D. C., Government Printing Office, 1961.
U. S. Bureau of Employment Security, BES No. U-203.

205. "Unemployment Insurance in the USA, 1956-1960," *Employment
Security Review*, XXVII (August, 1960), 1-38.

206. "Unemployment Insurance Legislation in 1961," *Monthly Labor
Review*, LXXXIV (December, 1961), 1350-55.

207. *Unemployment Insurance Schemes.* Geneva, International Labour Office, 1955.
208. R. G. Wagenet. "Twenty-five Years of Unemployment Insurance in the United States," *Social Security Bulletin,* XXIII (August, 1960), 50-59.
209. Wages and Related Benefits, 19 Labor Markets, 1957-58. Washington, D. C., Government Printing Office, 1959. U. S. Bureau of Labor Statistics.
210. H. M. Wagner. "A Reappraisal of Experience Rating," *Southern Economic Journal,* XXV (April, 1959), 459-69.
211. R. C. Wilcock. "Women in the American Labor Force: Employment and Unemployment," in Studies in Unemployment, pp. 121-72. Washington, D. C., Government Printing Office, 1960. Prepared for the Special Committee on Unemployment Problems, U. S. Senate, 86th Cong., 2d sess.
212. Elizabeth C. Wilson. "UI and the Stability of Wages in Great Britain," *International Labour Review,* XXX (December, 1934), 767-96.
213. W. S. Woytinsky. Additional Workers and the Volume of Unemployment in a Depression. Washington, D. C., Social Science Research Council, 1940. Pamphlet Series No. 1.

STATISTICAL SOURCES AND GENERALLY USEFUL PERIODICALS

214. *Bulletin of the International Social Security Association.*
215. Current Population Reports: Population Characteristics. U. S. Bureau of the Census, Series P-20, No. 109, July 17, 1961.
216. Current Population Reports: Population Characteristics. U. S. Bureau of the Census, Series P -20, No. 113, January 22, 1962.
217. Economic Report of the President. Washington, D. C., Government Printing Office. Annual.
218. *Employment Security Review.*
219. *Industry and Labor.*
220. *International Labour Review.*
221. *The Labor Market and Employment Security.*
222. *Social Security Bulletin.*
223. *Statistical Yearbook.* United Nations. (Annual.)
224. *Statistics of Sources and Uses of Finances, 1948-1958.* Organization for European Economic Cooperation, Paris, 1960.
225. *Survey of Current Business.*
226. U. S. Census of Population, 1960: United States Summary, General Social and Economic Characteristics. Washington, D. C., Government Printing Office, 1962. U. S. Bureau of the Census, PC(1)1C.

AUTHOR INDEX

SUBJECT INDEX

Aged, *see* Elderly persons

Anderson-King legislation, 60

Area Redevelopment Act of 1961, 77, 98–99

Australia, social security contributions, 22; social security expenditures, 15, 19

Austria, obligatory social security, 21; social security expenditures, 14–15, 18

"Automatic stabilizers," 4, 75, 86, 88–89

Belgium, earnings-related benefits, 20; obligatory social security, 21; social security expenditures, 15, 18

Benefits, as related to wages: foreign programs, 20, 58, 86; and unemployment, 100–2; *see also* OASDI, Unemployment insurance

Beveridge Report, 56

Canada, social security contributions, 22; social security expenditures, 14–15, 19

Ceylon, social security expenditures, 15, 19

Chile, social security expenditures, 15, 19

China (Taiwan), social security expenditures, 15, 19

Committee on Economic Security, 100

Common Market, 22; unemployment benefits of, 86

Consumption, by aged, 58–60; in Great Britain, 49; and income, 47, 79–86; and OASDI, 44–52, 75; patterns of, 51–53, 55; theory of, 45–52, 67–68, 75, 82

Countercyclical effects, of OASDI, 53–55, 75; of unemployment compensation, 86–89

"Cyclically graduated compensation," 102–3, 115

Denmark, income redistribution, 29–30; obligatory social security, 22; social security expenditures, 15, 18

Depression, 3; of 1930s, 6–7, 10, 35; countercyclical effects of, 54, 86–89

Disability insurance, 39, 119; temporary expenditures, 8, 10

Dissaving, 45–48

Earnings, *see* Wages

Elderly persons, consumption patterns of, 58–60; dissaving by, 48–49; geographic mobility of, 53; housing for, 53, 59–60, 63; income disparities, 62; income status of, 40–43; medical care for, 52, 59–60, 63, 105; participation in labor force, 31–40; poverty of, 1, 40; special services for, 63; tax privileges of, 63